100
GREAT
AMERICAN
PARKS

100 GREAT AMERICAN PARKS

STEPHANIE PEARSON

FOREWORD BY GARTH BROOKS

NATIONAL GEOGRAPHIC

WASHINGTON, D.C.

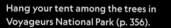

Hang your tent among the trees in Voyageurs National Park (p. 356).

PAGES 2–3: A weather-beaten pine grows through the cracks in glacier-polished granite at Olmsted Point, a majestic lookout over Yosemite National Park (p. 64).

CONTENTS

★★★★★★★★★★★★★★★★★★★★★★★

FOREWORD

BY GARTH BROOKS

★★★★★★★★★★★★★★★★★★★★★★★★

I've been fortunate in my life to travel extensively around this great country of ours. As a touring musician, I've been to busy cities, performed stadiums where the mountains peeked up behind the crowd, and visited towns so small that you'd be hard-pressed to find them on a map. In every state, city, and town, at every diner, motel, and truck stop, one thing is clear—the story of America lives in the land. The American land is as diverse as its people. From the forests of the Northwest to the beaches of Florida, from the deserts of the Southwest to the rocky coastline of New England, most people have barely scratched the surface when it comes to all America has to show.

The parks in these pages—100 in total, including all 63 national parks—are a testament to the unique and amazing landscapes around us, as well as to the many people who call this land their home. Some parks protect precious and vulnerable habitats, some serve as reminders of important events from our history, and others provide a serene space for visitors to transition from go, go, going all the time to just ... being. And you know why? Whether staring across the rippled, salty surface of Death Valley; feeling tiny, tucked up against the trunk of a giant sequoia; or hiking through the famous blue fog of the Great Smoky Mountains, getting out into nature helps put things in perspective. It reminds us of our place on the planet. It's a harbor for the soul.

This book is both a celebration and an invitation. The parks featured here honor America's magnificent landscapes as well as the country's complex and storied history. Paired with stunning photography, every entry will inspire and encourage you to get out and explore, to experience places you've never been, and to look with fresh eyes at our blessed United States of America. ■

Herds of bison regularly make their way through the northern range of Yellowstone National Park (p. 88).

INTRODUCTION

★★★★★★★★★★★★★★★★★★★★★★★

The park of my childhood was 660 acres (267.1 ha) of wild space that began at the end of the street where I grew up in Duluth, Minnesota. In 1941, the city cleared this onetime farm of buildings and claimed it as a park. With dense forests, swamps, and even a small "mountain" with views to passing ships on Lake Superior, it was like my own kid-size personal wilderness.

We all need a space to feel free. It can be in the form of an urban oasis like New York City's Central Park (p. 244), a regional state park like Rhode Island's Fort Adams (p. 250), or an exotic once-in-a-lifetime destination like Denali National Park in Alaska (p. 162). As writer and conservationist Wallace Stegner once famously wrote, "National parks are the best idea we ever had. Absolutely American, absolutely democratic, they reflect us at our best rather than our worst."

The story of how America's parks came to be, however, isn't as clear-eyed and altruistic as Stegner implies. The more I researched this book, the more I realized that to celebrate parks only for the beauty, joy, and solace they provide would be telling a mere fraction of the story.

The first park in the United States, Boston Common, wasn't initially a place to relax. In 1634, the Puritan founders of the Massachusetts Bay Colony used the 50-acre (20.2 ha) space to graze cows. More than a century later the British redcoats occupied the Common to use as a military encampment. And until 1817, an old elm tree in its center was the site of public hangings. In the 1960s, Martin Luther King, Jr., spoke to thousands from a podium in the park, demanding racial justice, a cry that rang out again during the Black Lives Matter demonstrations in the summer of 2020. Today the park offers space to recreate, exercise, and enjoy life, but it's also a memorial to the many Americans who have sacrificed over four centuries in our nation's continual fight for freedom.

In 1872, Congress established Yellowstone National Park in the territories of Wyoming and Montana as a "public park or pleasuring-ground for the benefit and enjoyment of the people." The first national park in the world, Yellowstone sparked a global conservation movement that has resulted in more than 100 nations protecting more than 1,200 national parks and preserves.

The less publicized side of the story is that when Yellowstone became a park, officials heavily discouraged the presence of Indigenous tribes because they believed they would frighten away tourists. The lands Yellowstone encompassed,

Come fall, New Hampshire's White Mountains (p. 236) are capped by snow, while the trees burst with autumnal hues.

The U.S. Virgin Islands offer parks of the tropical variety, particularly surrounding Caneel Bay on St. John (p. 210).

however, had been a home, seasonal migration path, or important spiritual site for dozens of tribes for, in some cases, thousands of years. The same story of the displacement of Indigenous peoples repeats itself over and over and over again in the development of the national parks across the United States.

Established in 1916, the U.S. National Park Service manages more than 420 units across 85 million acres (34.4 million ha). All 63 national parks are included in this book, as well as 37 other equally compelling places—at least one in every state, territory, and district in the union. Some are, admittedly, loose definitions of the word "park." Those include historical sites, wildlife refuges, and congressionally designated wilderness areas. But every destination in this book educates and inspires. Throughout, we describe the complex history of these treasured places, as well as what you can do and see within each park if you are fortunate enough to visit.

Everyone deserves a place to experience beauty and feel the peace that open spaces bring. But we also have a responsibility to educate ourselves about the past and to be better stewards of the land and to each other. If shown the proper respect, these parks will last for generations to come. I hope this book inspires you to take on that stewardship. ■

Red-rock formations dot the landscape of Bryce Canyon (p. 124), a stunning display of geological forces across millennia.

PART ONE

THE WEST & THE PACIFIC

Saguaro National Park (p. 24) gets its name from the species of giant, branched cacti, which can grow as tall as 50 feet (15.2 m).

PETRIFIED FOREST NATIONAL PARK

★★★★★★★★★★★★★★★★★★★★★★★★★

Thousands of vehicles speed cross-country on Interstate 40 in northeastern Arizona every day, their drivers mesmerized by the flat-topped mesas and wind-sculpted buttes of the Painted Desert. What many travelers don't realize, however, is that an easy exit off the interstate brings them to a national park that contains natural history dating back to the Triassic period and human history of the Paleo-Indian people who lived at the end of the last ice age.

There are more than 800 archaeological and historical sites in Petrified Forest National Park, but the primary attraction is its 200-million-year-old trees. These conifers, some 200 feet (61 m) tall, washed into an ancient river system and were buried by massive mounds of sediment. Over hundreds of thousands of years, silica from volcanic ash replaced the organic matter in the logs and eventually crystallized into sparkling quartz. These quartz logs are so dense, weighing up to 200 pounds (90.7 kg) per cubic foot, that ancestral Puebloan people used them to build homes like the reconstructed Agate House, estimated to have been used between 1050 and 1300.

The park contains many surprises, like Newspaper Rock, so named for more than 650 petroglyphs in one area. The ancient site was used by Puebloans between 650 and 2,000 years ago. Modern American Indians interpret them as clan symbols, a calendar, or markings of spiritual significance. ■

SIZE OF PARK: 229.6 square miles (594.6 sq km) ★ **BEST TIME TO GO:** Year-round
YEAR ESTABLISHED: 1962 ★ **IN-PARK ACCOMMODATIONS:** Camping

Large and colorful petrified logs and stumps dot the landscape of the national park.

GRAND CANYON NATIONAL PARK

★★★★★★★★★★★★★★★★★★★★★★★★★

There's no better place than the Grand Canyon to make one feel like a speck of dust in the continuum of the universe. To hike into the red canyon, take in the multicolored geologic layers from Yavapai Point, see a California condor soar above its walls, float the mighty Colorado River, or watch the sun rise or set at Hopi Point is to experience a sacred connection to place that humans have felt for 12,000 years.

One mile deep (1.6 km), 277 river miles (445.8 km) long, and averaging 10 miles (16.1 km) across rim to rim, this yawning chasm in Earth's crust exposes rock that formed 1.8 billion years ago. The canyon itself is young by comparison, having been formed five to six million years ago, when erosion from the Colorado River cut a deep channel through the Colorado Plateau, slicing through 19 distinct rock formations, some of which are hundreds of feet deep. Geologists call this process of a river carving out a canyon "downcutting."

The Grand Canyon's human history is as varied and as distinctive as its geology. Today there are 11 Traditionally Associated Tribes and historic ethnic groups whose people, over millennia, have lived in or near the Grand Canyon. Of the park's 4,615 archaeological resources (only 6 percent of the park has been intensively surveyed so far), the oldest are stone spear points that date back to the Paleo-Indians of the last ice age, a time when giant sloths and mammoths still roamed the earth.

SIZE OF PARK: 1,904 square miles (4,931 sq km) ★ **BEST TIME TO GO:** Year-round
YEAR ESTABLISHED: 1919 ★ **IN-PARK ACCOMMODATIONS:** Lodges & camping

The hike along the base of the canyon to Supai Village is 8 miles (12.9 km), followed by another 2 (3.2 km) to Havasu Falls.

HIDDEN TREASURE

In 1933, Civilian Conservation Corps workers discovered small figurines in a cave, shaped like deer or bighorn sheep, that were radiocarbon dated to between 2000 and 1000 B.C. Since the first discovery, hundreds more have been found in 10 other Grand Canyon caves. Anthropologists believe the figurines were carried by Indigenous people from the Archaic period to ensure a successful hunt.

In more recent human history, the Paiute, Navajo, Zuni, and Hopi tribes inhabited the Grand Canyon. The Havasupai, "people of the blue-green waters," so named for the nearby cerulean waterfalls, still live in the village of Supai, right outside the park, at the bottom of Havasu Canyon, one of the longest tributaries on the south side of the Grand Canyon. The tribe is intimately connected to this land and water. Its

Just beyond Grand Canyon National Park's borders, Havasupai Indian Reservation is home to the stunning Havasu Falls.

more than 500 members own a lodge and campground that hosts almost 20,000 visitors per year.

The Spanish conquistadores were the first Europeans to reach the Grand Canyon in the 1540s. Three hundred years later the first U.S. explorer, Joseph Christmas Ives, led a mapping expedition down the Colorado River in 1858 via a 54-foot (16.5 m) stern wheel steamboat of his own design. He made it as far as the Black Canyon but aborted the mission there, deterred by a quick succession of seemingly impassable rapids. A decade later, in 1869, John Wesley Powell, the geologist and Civil War veteran, led nine men down the river in four wooden dories. The first documented descent of the Colorado River through the Grand Canyon was a wild ride, one that led to damaged boats, food rations lost to the water, and desertion by an expedition member. That infamous journey and a subsequent expedition in 1871 provided the first accurate maps of the Colorado River.

Today, fewer than 5 percent of the park's five million annual visitors drop below the rim of the Grand Canyon. Of those 5 percent, some wait years to draw a non-commercial river permit in the annual lottery. Others sign on with a licensed outfitter for a raft trip. Still others stay at Phantom Ranch, the only lodge below the rim tucked at the bottom of the canyon on the shoreline of Bright Angel Creek. The peaceful oasis, designed in 1922 by architect Mary Jane Colter, was an inspiring getaway for artists and writers. To this day, the only way to reach it is by raft, mule, or on foot. ∎

Paddle through the canyon on the Colorado River rapids.

HIKE OF A LIFETIME

Of the roughly five million people who visit the Grand Canyon every year, fewer than one percent descend the grueling 14.6-mile (23.5 km), 5,850-foot (1,783.1 m) North Kaibab Trail to the bottom of the canyon, then hike the 9.6 miles (15.5 km) and 4,460 feet (1,359.4 m) back up the other side on the Bright Angel Trail. The hike is intense, but the reward is trekking through 11 layers of rock and two billion years of geologic history.

The Grand Canyon stretches
10 miles (16.1 km) wide,
277 miles (445.8 km) long,
and a mile (1.6 km) deep.

SAGUARO NATIONAL PARK

★ ★

I t's unusual to find such a wild national park so close to a large urban center. Eighty percent of this Sonoran Desert landscape is wilderness, despite the fact that the city of Tucson bisects its two sections: Saguaro West, which provides low-desert views of the Tucson mountains, and Saguaro East, which includes the pine-covered summits of the Rincon Mountains, which rise to a height of 8,666 feet (2,641.4 m). Both sections of the park are essential to the survival of its eponymous species, the saguaro cactus, a symbol of the American West.

For thousands of years, the Tohono O'odham people have been harvesting the fruit from the saguaro in what is now the national park. In their ancient stories, the saguaro was a human being who turned into a cactus, and as such, it needs to be cared for and respected. The Tohono O'odham still harvest the fruit, but only after animals have taken what they need to ensure that the saguaro's seeds are properly dispersed throughout the desert. More than 100 species of plants, reptiles, insects, and mammals use the cactus for food or shelter.

In the 1920s, University of Arizona president Homer Shantz led a movement to preserve the saguaro, which was being decimated by industrial ranchers whose cattle overgrazed the vulnerable desert. In his words, he set out to create

SIZE OF PARK: 142.9 square miles (370 sq km) ★ BEST TIME TO GO: Year-round
YEAR ESTABLISHED: 1933 ★ IN-PARK ACCOMMODATIONS: Camping

The two sections of Saguaro National Park border the city of Tucson.

"a great natural area for maintaining the botanical and zoological forms of the Southwest under natural conditions."

Shantz got his wish in 1933 when Herbert Hoover designated Saguaro National Monument 15 miles (24.1 km) east of what was then the sleepy town of Tucson. Over the years, the monument boundaries expanded, and in 1994, it became a national park. Today, thanks to a large-scale study

The Gila monster, one of two venomous lizards in the world, is native to the Arizona desert landscape.

Ancient stone art can be found throughout the park.

Flower clusters emerge from the tips of the saguaro cactus limbs.

and monitoring system that began in 1941, the park maintains a healthy population of saguaro. The greatest threats to this iconic cactus are the increasing temperatures due to climate change and the increasing impact of the growing city on the fragile desert.

Beyond the saguaro, the park is a fascinating place to hike and absorb the wonder of the Sonoran ecosystem, observing plants and animals that can seemingly miraculously survive despite limited water, animals like the desert tortoise, which stores water in its bladder; the Gila monster, which lives off the fat in its tail; and the javelina, which is able to hydrate by digesting the prickly pear cactus. ∎

“ More than 100 species of plants, reptiles, insects, and mammals use the cactus for food or shelter. ”

DEATH VALLEY NATIONAL PARK

★ ★

Death Valley National Park boasts an impressive number of superlatives: In 1913, the hottest temperature on Earth, 134°F (56.6°C), was recorded here. The record still stands, but in 2020, the park recorded a searingly close temperature of 130°F (54.4°C). Death Valley also contains both the lowest elevation in North America, 282 feet (86 m) below sea level, and peaks that rise higher than 11,000 feet (3,352.8 m).

Because four mountain ranges separate it from the moisture of the Pacific Ocean, Death Valley receives less than two inches (5.1 cm) of rain per year. As if owning the hottest, lowest, and driest national park in the country title weren't enough, it's also the largest national park in the lower 48, surpassing even Yellowstone.

This seemingly inhospitable landscape was deemed Death Valley by a prospecting expedition that lost one of its men here in 1849 while making their way west to the gold rush. The name is a bit of a misnomer, however: People, flora, and fauna have thrived in this arid landscape for centuries. Ancestors of the Timbisha Shoshone tribe arrived in the region a thousand years ago, harvesting piñon pine nuts and mesquite beans; hunting bighorn sheep, rabbits, and lizards; and finding pure water sources at springs. And what the prospectors named a "valley" is, in fact, not a valley at all. It's a 140-mile-long (225.3 km) graben, a geological term for a depressed block of Earth's crust that is bordered by parallel faults.

SIZE OF PARK: 5,270 square miles (13,649 sq km) ★ **BEST TIME TO GO:** October to April
YEAR ESTABLISHED: 1994 ★ **IN-PARK ACCOMMODATIONS:** Lodges & camping

Patterns in the salt flats stretch out over Death Valley as a storm clears.

Along hiking trails near Zabriskie Point, take in otherworldly rock formations caused by erosion.

In the mid-1800s, as mining in the region picked up, Death Valley was the wildest epicenter of the Wild West, with prospectors mining for gold, silver, lead, zinc, and many other precious metals. In its heyday in the early 1900s, the nearby town of Rhyolite had as many as 50,000 residents, 50 saloons, 18 stores, two churches, two undertakers, an opera house, and a red-light district.

Perhaps the toughest character of all to cross Death Valley was Juliet Brier, a member of the famed '49ers gold-prospecting expedition. The five-foot-tall (1.5 meters), 90-pound (40.8 kilogram) woman was known as the "best man in the party," for singlehandedly hauling water, cooking food, and loading and unloading the oxen.

Today, extremists time their trip to coincide with the hottest days of summer in order to snap a selfie with the record-breaking temperatures recorded on the outdoor thermometer at the Furnace Creek Visitor Center. A more hospitable time to visit is in the cooler months (October to May), when a hike on the Badwater salt flats under a full moon is not only possible, but also deeply illuminating. ∎

CLIMATE CHANGE REALITY CHECK

In 2020, the park experienced some of the hottest temperatures recorded on Earth. The August 16 high mark of 130°F (54.4°C) was the hottest temperature the world has seen since 1931. On August 17, the average daily temperature of 115.5°F (46.4°C) tied for the hottest daily average temperature ever recorded.

JOSHUA TREE NATIONAL PARK

★ ★

This arid landscape of exposed granite monoliths, hazy mountain peaks, and meandering desert tortoises is most famous for its resident succulents named after the Old Testament prophet Joshua by Mormon settlers who thought the trees' branches appeared to be outstretched in prayer. But there's a lot more to this park than its Seussian trees: 140 miles (225.3 km) east of Los Angeles, Joshua Tree is where the Colorado and Mojave Deserts meet, making it an important ecosystem for a fascinating variety of flora.

More than 750 plant species have been documented here. And because of all that plant life, animals like desert iguanas, golden eagles, mountain lions, and roadrunners thrive here.

Many national parks are associated with a rugged outdoorsman who was instrumental in the park's establishment: Yosemite has John Muir; Yellowstone has Ferdinand Hayden; and Rocky Mountain has Enos Mills. But a genteel woman is largely responsible for creating Joshua Tree National Park. Minerva Hamilton Hoyt was a transplanted southern socialite who became a passionate gardener when she moved to Pasadena with her husband. The more time Hoyt spent in the nearby desert, the more she recognized its austere beauty, as well as the rapid destruction of fragile desert plants by people who were digging them up or, worse, burning

SIZE OF PARK: 1,235 square miles (3,199 sq km) ★ BEST TIME TO GO: September to May
YEAR ESTABLISHED: 1994 ★ IN-PARK ACCOMMODATIONS: Camping

Stay in Joshua Tree for epic sunsets of pink, blue, purple, and yellow descending over a field of trees.

them. To better preserve the flora, she founded the International Deserts Conservation League and hired biologists and desert ecologists who helped prepare reports that, ultimately, President Franklin D. Roosevelt used to establish Joshua Tree as a national monument in 1936. Mount Minerva Hoyt, a 5,405-foot (1,647.4 m) peak in the west central portion of the park, is named in the pioneering preservationist's honor.

Hikers, rock climbers, campers, and birders flock to Joshua Tree for its 300 miles (482.8 km) of hiking trails, 4,500 established climbing routes, and abundance of backcountry camping options—85 percent of the park is managed as wilderness.

> **"** Many national parks are associated with a rugged outdoorsman … But a woman is largely responsible for creating Joshua Tree. **"**

Though known for its trees, the national park also boasts desert landscapes across its Hidden Valley.

Massive rocks and other formations dot the landscape of Joshua Tree throughout the park.

Birders gravitate toward oases like Cottonwood Spring—an important water stop for gold prospectors, miners, and teamsters traveling through the region in the 1800s—where sightings might include greater roadrunners, mockingbirds, cactus wrens, mourning doves, Le Conte's thrashers, American kestrels, and red-tailed hawks.

The park recently earned a Silver Tier Designation from the International Dark-Sky Association, an impressive distinction for a park so close to urban centers like Palm Springs and Los Angeles that will help prevent light pollution from spreading into the desert. ∎

HISTORICAL FOOTNOTE

The Joshua Tree is a relic from the Pleistocene era, when giant ground sloths roamed the region. Dung from two types of sloths found in a cave outside of Las Vegas was found to have large amounts of tree seeds, leaves, and fruits. As a result, the sloths have been called the "Johnny Appleseeds" of the Joshua Tree, spreading its range.

KINGS CANYON NATIONAL PARK

★ ★

Groves of towering giant sequoias, Wild and Scenic–designated whitewater rivers, stunning granite outcrops of the High Sierra, marble-walled underground caves, and one of the deepest canyons in the country—this is what you'll find at Kings Canyon National Park. With roughly a third of the annual visitors of its iconic neighbor Yosemite National Park to the north, Kings Canyon is beloved by back-country hikers, whitewater kayakers, and those who want to immerse themselves in the largest expanse of contiguous wilderness in California.

Many visitors drive the Generals Highway, a 32.5-mile (53.3 km) road with steep switchbacks and stone bridges that connects Kings Canyon National Park to Giant Sequoia National Monument and its southerly neighbor Sequoia National Park. The road leads to the largest sequoia groves on Earth, where trees like the 268-foot (81.7 m) General Grant have stood for nearly two millennia.

Those who need more immersion will gravitate toward the east to the 93.3 percent of Sequoia and Kings Canyon National Parks that are designated as wilderness. Together the two parks, which are co-managed, contain a continuum of ecosystems that cover a greater range of vertical relief—from 1,370 to 14,405 feet (417.6–4,390.6 m) on top of Mount Whitney—than any

SIZE OF PARK: 722 square miles (1,869 sq km) ★ **BEST TIME TO GO:** May to June, September to October
YEAR ESTABLISHED: 1940 ★ **IN-PARK ACCOMMODATIONS:** Lodges & camping

Kings Canyon offers plenty of hiking, including the Rae Lakes Loop.

To understand how species diversity varies over time, scientists use specialized acoustical equipment to record soundscapes. In Kings Canyon, they've used this method in a variety of ways to learn, among other things, how wildfire affects bird populations; how the presence of non-native fish may change the variety of birds and bats foraging at lakes; and how species composition changes over years.

protected area in the lower 48. One of the best ways to experience it is to take a hike, like the 41.4-mile (66.6 km) Rae Lakes Loop, a series of three connected trails that climbs 7,000 feet (2,133.6 m) traveling through glacier-carved canyons, around turquoise lakes, and up to 11,978-foot (3,651 m) Glen Pass, where views to the scree-covered High Sierra slopes seem to go on forever.

Find majestic waterfalls throughout Kings Canyon.

Stand among giants in the Redwood Mountain Grove.

The Kearsarge Pinnacles are reflected at dusk in the lakes of Kings Canyon.

The world's most accomplished whitewater kayakers pilgrimage to the park at least once in their lifetime to attempt a descent of the Class V Middle Fork of the Kings. Paddling this federally designated National Wild and Scenic River requires an overnight wilderness permit that includes adjacent national forests, bear canisters for food storage, and a five-mile (8 km) portage over Bishop Pass to reach the put in. The payoff for the portage and subsequent extreme paddling—including boulder rapids with big holes and the necessity of portaging around even bigger rapids that are impossible to kayak—is camping under the shadow of Tchipite Dome, a jagged granite monolith that rises 3,500 feet (1,066.8 m) straight out of the glacially carved Tehipite Valley floor. ■

66 The world's most accomplished whitewater kayakers pilgrimage to the park at least once in their lifetime. 99

LASSEN VOLCANIC NATIONAL PARK

★★★★★★★★★★★★★★★★★★★★★★★★★

It's hard to fathom that every rock in Lassen originated from one of four types of volcanoes: shield, composite, cinder cone, or plug dome. The 10,457-foot (3,187.3 m) centerpiece of this dynamic landscape is Lassen Peak, a sacred mountain to the Atsugewi, Yana, Yahi, and Maidu people, who, over many centuries, used this area—abundant in deer, salmon, and acorns—for summer hunting, gatherings, and as a meeting point.

The ancient Maidu deemed the peak Kohm Yah-mah-nee, or "Snow Mountain," and centuries later, Lassen still receives some of the highest snowfalls in California. Lassen is one of only two volcanoes (the other being Mount St. Helens) in the lower 48 that was active in the 20th century. Its May 1915 eruption created an avalanche of melted snow and rock, devastating surrounding forests and raining ash 280 miles (450.6 km) to the east.

Visitors can witness the power of volcanic forces by hiking a portion of the park's 150 miles (241.4 km) of trails to sites like Boiling Springs Lake, where the water bubbles at 125°F (51.6°C); Bumpass Hell, where the landscape is alive with steaming fumaroles and bubbling mud pots; and Chaos Jumbles, the remains of a rock avalanche.

Because the park parallels past eruptions on Mars, astrobiologists from NASA's Ames Research Center are continuously researching its diverse thermal features and microbial populations that live within them in efforts to understand if microbial life could have existed on the red planet. ■

SIZE OF PARK: 166 square miles (429 sq km) ★ **BEST TIME TO GO:** Year-round
YEAR ESTABLISHED: 1916 ★ **IN-PARK ACCOMMODATIONS:** Lodges & camping

Lassen's Cinder Cone trail allows park visitors to explore the volcano, including the colorful Painted Dunes.

PINNACLES NATIONAL PARK

★★★★★★★★★★★★★★★★★★★★★★★

In the Gabilan Mountains, 120 miles (193.1 km) southeast of San Francisco, rust-colored spires rise into the sky. These pinnacles are what remain of 23-million-year-old volcanoes that erupted and flowed, then were torn apart by the Pacific Plate moving against the San Andreas Fault. Over millennia, wind and water eroded the rock and small streams carved steep canyons, some of which were filled in by giant boulders that created cave-like rooms and passageways under the rocks.

Thousands of years ago, this landscape was home to the Chalon and Mutsun people, but little is known about their life here. In 1791, the Spanish built Mission Soledad in the Salinas Valley, and for safety, many of the Native people tried to hide their identity and pass themselves off as Spanish. Their descendants still work with the park on eco-cultural restoration projects, like reintroducing Indigenous management techniques to reestablish native plants.

In the gold rush era, miners arrived to search for precious metals, but the rock didn't yield copper or gold. Local homesteaders, realizing the value of their unique landscape, began lobbying the government in the 1890s to preserve the spires and their surroundings. In 1908, President Theodore Roosevelt designated Pinnacles a national monument. Much of the park's infrastructure that is still in use today was built by a local group who called themselves the Pinnacle Boys.

SIZE OF PARK: 41.57 square miles (107.66 sq km) ★ BEST TIME TO GO: Weekdays, March to May
YEAR ESTABLISHED: 2013 ★ IN-PARK ACCOMMODATIONS: Camping

The 150-foot (45.7 m) Tiburcio's X is one of the more famous formations in the park.

There are three large faults within or near the park: Miner's Gulch, Pinnacles, and Chalone Creek. A seismometer along the still active Chalone Creek Fault records frequent small earthquakes in the park. The corresponding seismograph in the Bear Gulch Visitor Center allows visitors to see the nearly continuous series of small tremors and shakes.

This ancient, whimsical landscape is a fascinating place to explore, especially between the months of March and May, when 80 percent of the park's plants are in bloom: California poppies, fiesta flowers, shooting stars, monkey flowers, and others saturate the park with brilliant yellows, reds, oranges, and purples. As spring turns to summer, the lush garden turns into an arid desert landscape, where the days are hot but the nights

Gray pine trees, endemic to California, grow along the High Peaks Trail in Pinnacles.

Experience the otherworldly in Bear Gulch Cave.

Look to the skies to catch California condors in flight.

are vivid. Pinnacles' clear skies allow viewers to see constellations sparkle against the ink-black night.

In addition to stargazing, hiking, and rock climbing, the park is one of the only places in the world to experience the thrill of a soaring California condor. In 2003, Pinnacles became one of five release sites in western North America for captive-bred condors. With a wingspan of 9.5 feet (2.9 m), the largest land bird in North America can fly up to 200 miles (321.9 km) a day. In the 1980s, only 22 of these majestic birds remained in the wild. Today there are more than 300. ∎

66 This ancient, whimsical landscape is a fascinating place to explore, especially ... when the park's plants are in bloom. 99

REDWOOD NATIONAL AND STATE PARKS

★★★★★★★★★★★★★★★★★★★★★★★★★

In 1850, when loggers began to cut down trees in California, two million acres (809,371.3 ha) of ancient coast redwood forest sprawled across the northern part of the state. Today, 5 percent of that old-growth forest remains. The four parks just south of the Oregon border making up Redwood National and State Parks are working hard to preserve about half the ancient coast redwoods left in the entire world.

These conifers are an awe-inspiring national treasure. Some are more than 2,000 years old. And while they are not as voluminous as their giant sequoia cousins to the south in Sequoia and Kings Canyon National Parks, the tallest coast redwood ever recorded grew to a height of 379 feet (115 m), giving this species the distinction of being the tallest tree in the world.

The trees' magnificent height is largely thanks to northern California's ideal growing conditions: Between 60 and 140 inches (152.4–355.6 cm) of rain falls per year, and in the summer, fog rolls in from the Pacific, reducing evapotranspiration (evaporation from the land surface plus transpiration from plants). A temperate climate, rich soil from river bottom flats, and few natural enemies also contribute to its success. The tree itself has a few seemingly supernatural powers, including a tannin in the bark that makes it resistant to insects and burl sprouts, a hard conglomerate of dormant buds that act like scar tissue and promote growth after injury by fire. Like all healthy

SIZE OF PARK: 172 square miles (445 sq km) ★ **BEST TIME TO GO:** Year-round
YEAR ESTABLISHED: 1968 ★ **IN-PARK ACCOMMODATIONS:** Basic campground cabins & camping

Walk among giants in a redwood grove, where the tallest tree stands at 364 feet (111 m).

Redwood National and State Parks offer almost 70 miles (112.7 km) of interconnected coastal trail with five backcountry campsites. It winds from secluded sandy beaches up coastal bluffs through stands of Sitka spruce and old-growth redwood forest and down again to tide pools harboring crabs and sea stars along the wild Pacific Ocean.

ecosystems, the coast redwood isn't the only tree in the forest: In the parks' old-growth stands there are only about 12 coast redwoods per acre. Those are surrounded by a diverse and thriving population of hemlock, Douglas fir, and big-leaf maple trees, as well as a thick carpet of ferns covering the forest floor.

Old-growth coast redwoods are the main attraction here, but the interconnected series of

Preserving the natural landscape as much as possible, pathways have been cut through fallen tree trunks.

Breaking through the forest, the groves of the park open to rock-strewn beaches on the Pacific coast.

❝ The tallest coast redwood ever recorded grew to a height of 379 feet (115 m), giving this species the distinction of being the tallest tree in the world. ❞

parks has more than 200 miles (321.7 km) of trails that meander from sea level to 3,000 feet (914.4 m), from tidal pools and beaches to old-growth forest and prairie. One of three major river systems that flow through the park is the Smith, California's last major free-flowing waterway. It's one of 208 designated Wild and Scenic Rivers in the United States and is an important habitat for salmon and steelhead trout. It's also a legendary destination for whitewater paddlers who want to experience the fickle unpredictability of an undammed river. ∎

SEQUOIA NATIONAL PARK

★ ★

In 1890, when President Benjamin Harrison designated Sequoia as the second national park in the country, the primary objective was to protect its majestic namesake species from wildfires and logging. The mandate wasn't as straightforward as it may have seemed. Unbeknownst to scientists and conservationists at the time, low-intensity fires are essential to the massive conifers' reproduction—their heat releases the trees' seeds and clears the ground of detritus to allow the dropped seedlings to more easily take root.

Additionally, this mountainous wilderness on the western slope of the Sierra Nevada was so undeveloped that it was a challenge to keep out illegal poachers and loggers. To change that, then-captain Charles Young, a Black man born into enslavement in Kentucky, led his 96-man unit of Buffalo Soldiers into the park as its acting super-intendent for the summer of 1903. In a few months' time, the hardworking soldiers finished a road that would lead to the sequoia groves, opening up the park for its intended purpose of tourism.

Visitors today largely have Colonel Young and his soldiers to thank for access to the Giant Forest, the largest of the unlogged giant sequoia groves on the planet. Here they can stand in awe under the General Sherman Tree, the world's largest tree by volume, standing 275 feet (83 m) tall and measuring 36 feet (11 m) in diameter at its base. ■

SIZE OF PARK: 631 square miles (1,634 sq km) ★ **BEST TIME TO GO:** June to October
YEAR ESTABLISHED: 1890 ★ **IN-PARK ACCOMMODATIONS:** Lodges & camping

A team of scientists measure the circumference of a giant sequoia.

GOLDEN GATE NATIONAL RECREATION AREA

★★★★★★★★★★★★★★★★★★★★★★★★★★

Most of us think of Golden Gate National Recreation Area (GOGA) as the grounds on either side of the iconic orange 2.7-mile-long (4.3 km) suspension bridge that stretches across San Francisco Bay. But the park is exponentially larger, sprawling from Marin County's Tomales Bay in the north 87 miles (140 km) south to Phleger Estate, a serene woodland in San Mateo County.

Across its 37 separate sites, GOGA has five lighthouses, 12 sand beaches, 78 shipwrecks, 146 miles (235 km) of trails, 1,439 historic structures, and 36,000 volunteers to assist its 15 million annual visitors. In one day, it's possible to ferry into San Francisco Bay to tour Alcatraz, the one-time maximum-security prison known as "the Rock" that held criminals like Al Capone; throw a

Frisbee in Crissy Field under the shadow of the Golden Gate Bridge; then drive over the bridge to hike to the Muir Beach Overlook and spot whales in the Pacific. And those sites are only a mere fraction of the park.

The establishment of this diverse, urban wonderland in 1972 is the result of citizens standing up for open spaces. In the rapid post–World War II

SIZE OF PARK: 129.36 square miles (335 sq km) ★ **BEST TIME TO GO:** Year-round
YEAR ESTABLISHED: 1972 ★ **IN-PARK ACCOMMODATIONS:** Lodges & camping

Stroll along Marshall's Beach at the Presidio in Golden Gate NRA.

development era of the 1950s and 1960s, San Francisco was at risk of being consumed by urban sprawl. As a result, more than 60 Bay Area activist groups banded together to form People for a Golden Gate National Recreation Area. Their momentum, in conjunction with the 19-month occupation of the former Alcatraz prison by an Indigenous American group known as Indians of All Tribes in 1969, brought the issue of creating public spaces for all to the attention of the Nixon

Alcatraz operated as a federal penitentiary for 29 years and can now be toured.

administration. In 1972, with bipartisan support, Nixon signed "An Act to Establish the Golden Gate National Recreation Area."

The park is best known for the bridge, the old-growth redwoods of Muir Woods in Marin County on one side, and the 1,500-acre (607 ha) Presidio, a former U.S. Army military fort that juts out the northern tip of the San Francisco Peninsula on the other. But more recent additions include Rancho Corral de Tierra, a 4,000-acre (1,618.7 ha) portion of a Mexican land grant that is still largely undeveloped open space of grasslands and ranches on the San Mateo County coastline south of San Francisco. The rolling hills with hazy views to the Pacific are habitat for several rare and endangered flora and fauna including peregrine falcons, the San Bruno elfin butterfly, and the brilliant yellow Hickman's cinquefoil flower. One spectacular and steep hike here is the mile-long (1.6 km) power ascent up 2,000-foot (609.6 m) Montara Mountain, with rewarding views to the Farallon Islands at the top.

A delightful way to while away an afternoon in San Francisco is to play, picnic, and explore the

A white-crowned sparrow perches at Fort Point.

Presidio fort, which dates back to 1776. Start at the fully refurbished century-old guardhouse, the William Penn Mott, Jr., Presidio Visitor Center in the Main Post area. Nearby, in the historic Powder Magazine, a storeroom built during the Civil War to house army munitions, Andy Goldsworthy's "Tree Fall" is on display. The eucalyptus tree removed from the Presidio Parkway and preserved in cracked clay is one of four Goldsworthy pieces in the park. An exciting addition to the Presidio is the 14-acre (5.7 m) Tunnel Tops project, expected to be completed by the spring of 2022. It adds new green spaces over existing highway tunnels, giving visitors even more extensive and awe-inspiring views to the Golden Gate Bridge. ∎

HIKE OF A LIFETIME

Six miles (9.7 km) of trails meander through the Muir Woods, a 558-acre (225.8 ha) forest north of the Golden Gate Bridge. A portion of the trees here are old-growth redwoods that soar as high as 258 feet (78.6 m) and are 600 to 800 years old, teenagers compared to the oldest-living coastal redwoods, which are 2,200 years old.

From the Muir Beach Overlook, 30 miles (48.3 km) north of San Francisco, take in sweeping views of the Pacific Ocean.

CHANNEL ISLANDS NATIONAL PARK

★★★★★★★★★★★★★★★★★★★★★★★★

Islands have always captured the human imagination, as evidenced by centuries worth of best-selling literature using their mystique as a backdrop from Daniel Defoe's 1719 faux autobiography *Robinson Crusoe* to Jules Verne's 1875 novel *The Mysterious Island* to William Golding's 1954 classic *Lord of the Flies*. The Channel Islands are no exception. These five Pacific islands that compose the national park were formed by volcanic activity 14 million years ago.

They sit just offshore of populous Southern California, yet their coastlines remain undeveloped and surrounded by one of the most productive marine environments in the world. Home to nearly 150 endemic species, Channel Islands National Park is often referred to as the "Galápagos of North America."

The Santa Barbara Channel, the body of water that separates the mainland from the Channel Islands, supports more than 1,000 marine species, from plankton to blue whales. Because of this diversity, Jacques Cousteau listed the Channel Islands as one of the premier dive spots in the world. Its giant kelp forests, where golden hues of sunlight shine through, support abundant life like bright orange garibaldi and giant sea bass.

Anacapa, the closest to the mainland of the park's islands, sits just 11 nautical miles (17.7 km) off the Ventura County coastline, but the Channel Islands were never connected to the mainland. It's

SIZE OF PARK: 390 square miles (1,010 sq km) ★ BEST TIME TO GO: Year-round
YEAR ESTABLISHED: 1980 ★ IN-PARK ACCOMMODATIONS: Camping

Take the trail above
Scorpion Beach for coastal
sunrise and sunset views.

surprising then that one of the oldest-known human remains in North America was found on Santa Rosa Island in 1959. The discovery supports growing evidence that not all of North America's original inhabitants migrated from the Bering Land Bridge that once connected Asia with North America. Instead, many anthropologists and archaeologists believe that the first North

The park's iconic Arch Rock sits at one end of East Anacapa Island.

Americans followed an ice-free coastal route along the Pacific Rim known as "the Kelp Highway," surviving off the resources these underwater forests produce. The islands' kelp forests are still some of the most robust in the world today, thanks to their isolation, a relative lack of pollution, and the confluence of ocean currents, which creates an upwelling of nutrients.

Until the early 1800s, roughly 1,200 Chumash people made their home on the northern Channel Islands. By the early 1800s, explorers, missionaries, and European settlers had decimated the population by passing on diseases like measles and exploiting the marine resources. The survivors were forced to move to the mainland Franciscan mission system in the 1820s. Two centuries later, however, their connection to their homeland remains strong. Every year, community members make the 17-mile (27.4 km) channel crossing from the mainland to Santa Cruz Island in a traditional *tomol,* a canoe like boat that they paddle.

Each Channel Island is spectacular in its own way—and all are open to the public. The farthest from the mainland, 9,500-acre (3,844.5 ha) San

The near threatened island fox is native to Santa Cruz.

Miguel, requires a 4.5-hour boat ride through oftentimes windy and foggy conditions. The payoff is a truly remote camping and hiking experience. The ranger-led, 16-mile (25.7 km) round-trip hike to Point Bennett—a peninsula jutting like a hammer into the ocean—yields views to a phenomenal site: tens of thousands of individual seals and sea lions, one of the largest concentrations of wildlife in the world.

Every season at the park brings its own beauty, whether the aroma of thousands of blooming wildflowers in spring, humpback whales feeding on krill off the coastlines in the summer, calm waters for kayaking in the fall, or wild solitude in the winter. ■

WILDLIFE SIGHTING

There are nearly 150 endemic species on the Channel Islands that are found nowhere else in the world. One of them is the island fox, a descendant of the mainland gray fox. The island fox is one of the smallest canid species in the world, a third the size of its mainland counterpart.

Wildflowers burst into bloom along the rocky coast-line of Santa Rosa Island.

YOSEMITE NATIONAL PARK

★ ★

Officially, Yosemite was the third national park to be established in the United States after Yellowstone and Sequoia National Parks. But this iconic California landscape of sheer granite walls, towering sequoia trees, and plunging waterfalls played a seminal role in the history of American conservation and the establishment of the National Park Service. Thousands of years before the first white men claimed to discover Yosemite Valley in 1851, it was home to the Ahwahneechee, a subtribe of the Miwok.

The lush vegetation and abundance of wildlife once supported 36 villages, the largest of which sat at the base of Yosemite Falls. But as was the case with so much of the American West, the local tribes clashed with the newcomers and were ultimately forced out by soldiers who were clearing the region for settlers and prospectors in search of gold.

Awed by the giant sequoias, some of the prospectors decided to prove the trees' existence to disbelieving folks back east. To do so, a group of enterprising men set about to remove the bark from the "Mother of the Forest," a giant sequoia tree—300 feet (91.4 ms) tall, 92 feet (28 m) in circumference, and about 2,500 years old. After 90 days, 60 tons of bark were removed, portions of

SIZE OF PARK: 1,169 square miles (3,027 sq km) ★ BEST TIME TO GO: May & October
YEAR ESTABLISHED: 1890 ★ IN-PARK ACCOMMODATIONS: Lodges & camping

The sun sets over El Capitan and the Merced River, two icons of Yosemite National Park.

PARK ICON

Alex Honnold's name goes hand in hand with Yosemite National Park. In June 2017, the American climber became the first and only person who has ever free-soloed 7,569-foot (2,307 m) El Capitan, which is considered one of the greatest athletic achievements in human history. He also holds the record for the fastest ascent of the Yosemite Triple Crown—Mount Watkins, the Nose, and the Regular Northwest Face of Half Dome—which he accomplished in 18 hours and 50 minutes.

which were sent to New York and London as a P. T. Barnum–esque carnival attraction. The plan to enthrall backfired. Much of the public was outraged by the desecration of the tree. To put a stop to the destruction, California senator John Conness sponsored the "Yosemite Grant," a bill that would save the Mariposa Grove of giant sequoias and the nearby Yosemite Valley.

On June 30, 1864, in the midst of the Civil War, President Abraham Lincoln signed the bill "upon the express conditions that the premises shall be

Yosemite Falls plummets 2,425 feet (739.1 m) from its upper falls to the base of the lower cascade.

held for public use, resort, and recreation." This act marked the first time a federal government set aside a piece of land purely for preservation for the people. Because there was no National Park Service then, the park was managed by the state of California. In 1890, lands surrounding Yosemite Valley and the Mariposa Grove were designated a national park. Almost two decades later, in 1906 after a camping trip to the Yosemite backcountry with naturalist John Muir, President Theodore Roosevelt merged the state and public-managed lands into the current park. The trip concretized Roosevelt's vision for the National Park Service, which would be formally established in 1916 under President Woodrow Wilson.

Today, Yosemite is one of the most beloved national parks in the country, attracting an annual 4.5 million visitors. Its marquee attraction, Yosemite Valley, with the nearly 5,000-foot-high (1,524 m) granite walls of Half Dome and the cascade of Yosemite Falls plunging 2,425 feet (739.1 m) to the valley floor, makes up only 5 percent of the park. But there is so much more to see,

A rare sighting: Bobcats hunt throughout Yosemite.

ECOLOGICAL HIGHLIGHT

Yosemite is renowned for its waterfalls. The mightiest of all is Yosemite Falls, which is actually a chain of three waterfalls: Upper Yosemite Fall (1,430 feet/435.9 m), the middle cascades (675 feet/205.7), and Lower Yosemite Fall (320 feet/97.5 m). To see it from the top, hike the 7.2-mile (11.6 km) Yosemite Falls Trail, a strenuous route with a 2,700-foot (832 m) elevation gain.

such as Tuolumne Meadows, a subalpine valley intersected by the meandering Tuolumne River in the shadow of the High Sierra; three groves of ancient giant sequoias, including Mariposa, home to 500 of these behemoth trees; and Glacier Point, with its sweeping overlook of Yosemite Valley.

Behind Yosemite Museum is a reconstructed Ahwahnee village located on the former site of the largest Native American village in Yosemite Valley. It is used today by the local Native American community for ceremonies and special gatherings. ∎

Mist hangs over Dana Meadows just inside the Tioga Pass entrance of the park.

BLACK CANYON OF THE GUNNISON NATIONAL PARK

★★★★★★★★★★★★★★★★★★★★★★★★★

In 1853, a West Point Military Academy graduate, Capt. John W. Gunnison, led an expedition to find a navigable railroad route to the Pacific. In September, he reached the rim of a precipitous cliff over-looking what is now the Black Canyon of the Gunnison River, where he found "a stream imbedded in [a] narrow and sinuous canyon, resembling a huge snake in motion." The captain deemed the country "the roughest, most hilly and most cut up" he had ever seen.

The 48-mile-long (77.2 km) Black Canyon, which plunges 2,722 feet (829.7 m) at its deepest point, is not the deepest gorge in North America. That distinction goes to 8,043-foot (2,451.5 m) Hells Canyon in Idaho and Oregon. And it's not as deep as the Grand Canyon, which plunges 6,000 feet (1,828.8 m) at one point. Both of these deeper canyons have evidence of human habitation that dates back thousands of years. Black Canyon, however, has been nearly impenetrable to humans for time immemorial. With its two-billion-year-old sheer walls, plunging cliffs, and soaring buttresses, it was largely inaccessible even to the Ute, the oldest residents of Colorado, who still live in the

SIZE OF PARK: 48 square miles (121 sq km) ★ **BEST TIME TO GO:** Summer
YEAR ESTABLISHED: 1999 ★ **IN-PARK ACCOMMODATIONS:** Camping

Autumn hues color the forests of the Black Canyon of the Gunnison.

THE CHALLENGE

Kayaking the Black Canyon is for experts only. Most of the rapids in the park are Class V, and some sections are considered impassable. As if that weren't challenging enough, the river's water temperature is a cold 50°F (10°C) year-round and poison ivy grows as high as five feet (1.5 m) along its banks.

region today. Black Canyon's inaccessibility is the result of the near-vertical black gneiss walls and the powerful volume of water that the once undammed Gunnison River forced through the narrow canyon. At its narrowest point, the canyon floor is only 40 feet (12.2 m) wide.

Even today, the canyon presents formidable challenges for those who want to explore its

The Painted Wall is the tallest vertical cliff in Colorado, standing at 2,250 feet (685.8 m).

Yucca plants grow throughout the red landscape of the national park.

depths. There are no maintained or marked trails into the inner canyon, but intrepid souls can descend via a number of wilderness routes along the South Rim, like the 2.75-mile-long (4.4 km) Warner Route that drops 2,722 feet (829.7 m) and rewards its hikers with a mile (1.6 km) of riverbank access at a wider point in the canyon, an excellent perch from which to fly-fish for rainbow and brown trout.

For those who want to catch a glimpse similar to the one Captain Gunnison enjoyed nearly two centuries ago, an easy 200-yard hike from a pullout at the rim brings visitors to a majestic view of Painted Wall, which rises 2,250 feet (685.8 m) into the sky. So named for the pink pegmatite intrusions that stand out against the dark gneiss background, Painted Wall is the highest cliff in Colorado. ∎

❝ Black Canyon ... has been nearly impenetrable to humans for time immemorial. ❞

GREAT SAND DUNES NATIONAL PARK

★★★★★★★★★★★★★★★★★★★★★★★★

Drive north on arrow-straight Colorado 17 through the San Luis Valley in southeastern Colorado, and the tallest sand dunes in North America rise to the east, undulating 750 feet (228.6 m) into the sky like a hazy mirage. This massive expanse of volcanic sand spread across 28 square miles (72 sq km) is a surreal and beautiful sight to behold in the shadow of snowcapped fourteeners, one of which is 14,344-foot (4,372.1 m) Blanca Peak, a sacred mountain to the Navajo (Diné) people.

How the sand arrived in this high-alpine valley that sits 7,500 feet (2,286 m) above sea level involves numerous geologic processes. More than 100,000 years ago, an ancient lake sprawled across the valley floor. Rivers flowing down the mountainsides added to the sediment accumulation in the valley. Over thousands of years, the lake dried up and the predominant southwest winds funneled the sand toward a low curve in the Sangre de Cristo Mountains. From the east, opposing storm winds blew through three mountain passes stirring the sand upward into their present massive dunes.

In late August, bright yellow prairie sunflowers blanket the dunes, and in September, golden aspen flank the Sangre de Cristo Mountains as the Milky Way shimmers in the night sky. It's the ideal time to play in the sand, then pitch a tent at one of seven backcountry sites along the 11-mile-long (17.7 km) Sand Ramp Trail. ■

SIZE OF PARK: 169 square miles (437 sq km) ★ **BEST TIME TO GO:** August to September
YEAR ESTABLISHED: 2004 ★ **IN-PARK ACCOMMODATIONS:** Camping

Miles and miles of towering dunes—the tallest in North America—are the centerpiece of the park.

MESA VERDE NATIONAL PARK

★★★★★★★★★★★★★★★★★★★★★★★★★

There are many profoundly moving ancestral Puebloan sites across the Southwest: Bandelier National Monument in New Mexico's Frijoles Canyon and Navajo National Monument, hidden in Arizona's Tsegi Canyon, give visitors a sense of how essential the surrounding fortress-like canyons were in providing shelter from enemies and the elements. Chaco Culture National Historical Park, which sits in a wide, desolate valley, was once home to thousands of thriving residents.

Each of these sites is important for understanding the sophistication of ancestral Puebloan society. The largest of them all, and the largest archaeological preserve in the United States with more than 600 cliff dwellings, is Colorado's Mesa Verde National Park.

Of the 600 cliff dwellings at Mesa Verde, only four—Cliff Palace, Balcony House, Long House, and Step House—are open to the public on a regular basis. The largest of these, Cliff Palace, located at 7,000 feet (2,133.6 m), protected by an overhanging lip of the mesa above, seems an impossible architectural feat. The village, which is thought to have housed 100 residents, has roughly 150 rooms made from sandstone, mortar, and wood beams, and 21 round kivas, ceremonial underground rooms used for spiritual ceremonies. Based on its size, archaeologists speculate that Cliff Palace was likely the social and administrative epicenter of the region. The only way to see it up close is to

SIZE OF PARK: 81.25 square miles (210.43 sq km) ★ BEST TIME TO GO: May to June, September to October
YEAR ESTABLISHED: 1906 ★ IN-PARK ACCOMMODATIONS: Camping & lodges (summer only)

Cliff Palace, made of sandstone blocks, mortar, and wooden beams, is the well-preserved home of ancestral Puebloans.

Climate change is one of the factors causing the cliff dwellings to crumble. How much the National Park Service should intervene is an ongoing debate. The National Park Service's position is that they proactively maintain the four cliff dwellings that are open to the public for safety reasons. As for the others, they engage in active preservation (structural stabilization) and passive protection (legislated mandates and policy), but they do not actively rehabilitate the structures.

sign up for a ranger-led tour that involves climbing down 120 stone steps and up four ladders.

Because there are more than 5,000 archaeological sites being preserved on the grounds of Mesa Verde, from a scatter of pottery sherds to stone tool fragments to rubble mounds of collapsed walls and cliff dwellings, backcountry travel, camping, and hiking is not permitted. But there are trails, like the steep and rocky, 2.4-mile (3.9 km) Petroglyph Point Trail that leads to the largest

One of many structures, Pipe Shrine House was used from A.D. 900 to A.D. 1300.

Petroglyphs can be found throughout the Mesa Verde structures.

Visitors climb a ladder to view the Balcony House cliff dwelling.

66 There are more than 5,000 archaeological sites being preserved on the grounds of Mesa Verde. 99

panel of petroglyphs available to visitors. The meanings of the petroglyphs, which contain handprints and images of animals, have been lost to time, but one Hopi elder believes that the panel tells the story of two clans, the Sheep Clan and Eagle Clan, both of which separated from other people and returned to their place of origin. The boxy spiral on the petroglyph likely represents a *sipapu*, the place where the Pueblo Indians believe they emerged from the earth. ■

ROCKY MOUNTAIN NATIONAL PARK

★★★★★★★★★★★★★★★★★★★★★★★★★★

In 1879, British adventurer Isabella Bird wrote these words of the stunning landscape surrounding Estes Park in her newly published book, *A Lady's Life in the Rocky Mountains:* "I have dropped into the very place I have been seeking, but in everything it exceeds all my dreams ... The scenery is the most glorious I have ever seen, and is above us, around us, at every door."

Bird was no stranger to stunning places. She had traveled the world, was the first woman to be accepted into Great Britain's acclaimed Royal Geographical Society, and was the second woman to climb 14,259-foot (4,346.1 m) Longs Peak, the highest mountain in Colorado. Her words struck such a chord with her British readers that the book went "viral" and was soon being exported to France. By the turn of the century, tourists looking to find the scenery that Bird had described began to flock to Estes Park and its surroundings. In 1915, thanks to tireless lobbying by local naturalist and lodge owner Enos Mills, President Woodrow Wilson signed the Rocky Mountain National Park Act, creating the country's tenth national park.

Rocky Mountain National Park takes visitors' breath away in more ways than one: The park contains 77 peaks higher than 12,000 feet (3,657.6 m). Its 48-mile-long (77.2 km) Trail Ridge Road—a feat of engineering built in 1932 that winds between Grand Lake in the west and Estes Park

SIZE OF PARK: 415 square miles (1,074 sq km) ★ BEST TIME TO GO: June to September, December to March
YEAR ESTABLISHED: 1915 ★ IN-PARK ACCOMMODATIONS: Camping

A dusting of snow covers the trees and rocky ledges along a trail to Emerald Lake.

The Big Thompson River flows in front of the mountains making up the Continental Divide.

in the east—tops out at 12,000 feet (3,657.6 m), making it the highest continually paved road in the nation. With 358 square miles (927.2 sq km) managed as wilderness, there's room in the park for more than 60 mammal species including elk, moose, mountain lion, bighorn sheep, coyote, and black bear.

Today, roughly 4.5 million people visit the park each year, fulfilling Enos Mills's wish: "In years to come when I am asleep beneath the pines, thousands of families will find rest and hope in this park."

Families and individuals do find rest and hope in the park, hiking its 300 miles (482.8 km) of trails, fly-fishing for rainbow trout in mountain streams, attempting to summit mighty Longs Peak in the summer, or backcountry skiing the ample snow-laden slopes in the winter. With so many visitors, it's essential they thoughtfully read and take the Rocky Pledge, "to preserve unimpaired for this and future generations the beauty, history, and wilderness therein." ∎

CLIMATE CHANGE REALITY CHECK

In fall 2020, roughly 30,000 acres (12,140.7 ha)—or 9 percent—of Rocky Mountain National Park were burned by the East Troublesome and Cameron Peak Fires, the two largest wildfires in Colorado's history. The fires were fueled by drought, numerous dead trees killed by bark beetle infestations, and dry, windy conditions. These factors led to fire behavior that spread rapidly and out of control. Experts predict that the effects of climate change will contribute to increased occurrence of wildfires.

FRANK CHURCH RIVER OF NO RETURN WILDERNESS

★ ★

It is almost impossible to fathom the immensity of the largest contiguous wilderness in the lower 48, a roadless area that encompasses more than 2.5 million acres (1 million ha) of precipitous mountain peaks, free-flowing rivers, a gorge deeper than the Grand Canyon, and miles and miles of trees that span six different national forests in central Idaho. For campers, backcountry skiers, rock climbers, whitewater paddlers, hikers, fishermen, or anyone in search of true solitude, it's heaven.

Frank Church was an Idaho native and U.S. senator from 1957 to 1981 who was instrumental in the preservation of wilderness across the country. In 1964, Church sponsored the Wilderness Act, a bill signed by President Lyndon B. Johnson that today protects 110 million acres (44.5 million ha) in 44 states and Puerto Rico.

Four years later, Church introduced the Wild and Scenic Rivers Act. Today, it protects 208 rivers, including Idaho's Middle Fork of the Salmon, nicknamed the "River of No Return" more than a century ago because of the extreme difficulty in moving upstream against the fierce rapids and fast water.

SIZE OF PARK: 3,698.16 square miles (9,578.21 sq km) ★ BEST TIME TO GO: Year-round
YEAR ESTABLISHED: 1980 ★ IN-PARK ACCOMMODATIONS: None

A cave opening leads to a stunning view of Big Creek and the wilderness area.

THE CHALLENGE

The heart of the wilderness is the free-flowing, 104-mile-long (167.4 km) Middle Fork of the Salmon River, one of the most exhilarating paddling trips on the planet. With nonstop Class III to IV rapids, no dissecting roads, no Wi-Fi service, and no other amenities, this river trip is one of the last great off-the-grid adventures in the lower 48.

As devoid of humanity as it seems today, the Frank Church wilderness was home to the Tuka Deka, or Sheepeaters, until 1879. This branch of the western Shoshone tribe was renowned for its skill in hunting bighorn sheep. In the years leading up to 1879, the Sheepeaters were accused of an increasing number of crimes by local settlers, including stealing horses and murdering five

Take on the rapids of the Middle Fork of the Salmon River with experienced outfitters.

A coyote lets out a howl as dusk settles on the park.

Time your visit to take in the wildflowers at Loon Creek.

Chinese miners and two ranchers, despite the fact that there was no evidence backing up the charges. In 1879, U.S. Army general O. Howard dispatched Troop G of the First Cavalry to lead the investigation into the attacks. In May 1879, Troop G set out from Boise to track the nomadic tribe, spending four months marching up the Salmon River corridor in extreme weather, losing animals, ammunition, and supplies along the way. By October, after several skirmishes, the Army had succeeded in fending off attacks and even took hostages. The Sheepeaters surrendered, and most of the tribe was ultimately relocated to Fort Hall Reservation in southeastern Idaho. But Sheepeater history and culture is still very much alive in what is now protected wilderness area, especially along the Salmon River corridor, where alert visitors can see depressions from where their homes once sat and vivid pictographs that tell their stories. ■

YELLOWSTONE NATIONAL PARK

★★★★★★★★★★★★★★★★★★★★★★★★

Almost 150 years after its inception, the world's first national park remains a wonder. The Wild West landscape of mountains, rivers, canyons, hydrothermal features, lakes, and waterfalls sprawls across Wyoming, Montana, and Idaho, deriving its dynamic power from the underlying Yellowstone Volcano. This "supervolcano," believed to be the most powerful in the world, has fueled the park's more than 10,000 hydrothermal features for thousands of years.

With 500 active geysers, the park contains more than half of the world's total. Its iconic Old Faithful, one of the most predictable geysers on the planet, has erupted more than one million times since the park was born. There's a carnival atmosphere among the crowds who gather outside the stone-and-log Old Faithful Inn to gaze in slack-jawed wonder at the geyser, which shoots hot water up to 180 feet (54.9 m) in the air roughly 20 times per day.

The beauty of Yellowstone, however, is that there is so much more to the park than its most famous landmarks. It also contains the largest high-elevation lake in North America, the country's oldest and largest bison herd, and at least 1,800 archaeological sites from 26 associated Native American tribes. There is so much to explore here that a visit can seem overwhelming, especially in July, when the average visitation peaks at one million. The park is so beloved

SIZE OF PARK: 3,472 square miles (8,991 sq km) ★ **BEST TIME TO GO:** Summer, fall, winter
YEAR ESTABLISHED: 1872 ★ **IN-PARK ACCOMMODATIONS:** Lodges & camping

Yellowstone's Grand Prismatic Spring is the largest hot spring in the U.S.

In January and February, visitation to Yellowstone drops off to a fraction of summer visitation. Snow piles up, park entrances are blocked off, and visitors ski, snowmobile, or take a snowcoach tour into the park, for a near-private viewing of grazing, snow-covered buffalo and a much-less-crowded Old Faithful in full action.

As many as 5,500 bison roam through the national park.

that rangers encourage visitors to take a two-sentence promise known as the Yellowstone Pledge and to spread it wide on their social media feeds while in the park. Translated into 10 languages, the pledge is a reminder to visitors to take responsibility for their own actions while in the park, following important guidelines like staying on boardwalks in the hot thermal areas, carrying bear spray and knowing how to use it, and giving wildlife at least 75 feet (22 m) of space.

One of the most exciting reasons to visit the park is the opportunity to see wildlife. Yellowstone contains 67 mammal species including bison, black and grizzly bears, Canada lynx, coyote, wolves, mountain lions, mountain goats, and moose. It's the only place in the United States where bison have lived continuously since prehistoric times. The thousands of bison that still live here can be seen in almost every corner of the park, from the wide-open grasslands of the Lamar Valley near the park's northeast entrance, where they mingle with elk, moose, and bear, to the banks of the Madison River near the park's entrance at West Yellowstone. While the bison appear to be almost docile, minding their own business as they graze, every year there are reports of tourists being charged and, occasionally, stampeded by the ungulates made angry by invasive onlookers, so give them space.

In the height of the hot summer, Yellowstone Lake, which stretches 20 miles (32.2 km) long and

Despite its name, the Lower Falls, at 308 feet (93.9 m), is the tallest cascade in the park, more than twice the height of Niagara Falls.

14 miles (22.5 km) wide in almost the dead center of the park, looks inviting. But very few people attempt a swim because the average annual temperature is 41°F (5°C), freezing over in the winter with ice up to two feet (0.6 m) thick. The lake bottom, however, reaches depths of 390 feet (118.9 m) and is a largely unexplored thermal landscape of geysers, hot springs, and deep canyons. In Mary Bay, in the northeast corner of the lake, the water from an underwater hydrothermal vent was recently recorded at 252°F (122.2°C). Even underwater Yellowstone's dynamic volcanic landscape is constantly changing. ∎

BY THE NUMBERS: YELLOWSTONE

11,358: Highest point (in feet/3,461.9 m) on the summit of Eagle Peak

900: Miles (1,449 km) of hiking trails

1,000: Number of native flowering species

301: Number of backcountry campsites

25: Number of sites, landmarks, or districts on the National Register of Historic Places

16: Number of fish species

9: Number of lodges and hotels

2: Number of threatened species (Canada lynx and grizzly bears)

1: 630,000-year-old caldera

In the early morning hours, Castle Geyser releases steam in the Upper Geyser Basin.

GLACIER NATIONAL PARK

★★★★★★★★★★★★★★★★★★★★★★★★★

In 1895, the U.S. government sent treaty commissioners to the Blackfeet who lived in what is now Glacier National Park. After days of fruitless negotiations, the Blackfeet, who had recently survived one of the worst starvation winters in recent memory, finally ceded a portion of their homeland to the U.S. for $1.5 million. What the U.S. government received in return is one of the most singularly stunning and abundant alpine landscapes in the world.

More than 125 years later, the park, as part of the "Crown of the Continent" ecosystem that also includes the Bob Marshall Wilderness Complex to the west and Canada's Waterton Lakes National Park to the north, is still the most intact remaining temperate ecosystem in North America, where all the predators that were here before European settlement still remain.

Within park boundaries, there are 26 glaciers, 175 mountains (the highest of which, Mount Cleveland, rises to 10,448 feet/3,184.6 m), 762 lakes (the longest of which is 9.4-mile-long/15.1-km Lake McDonald), and 2,865 miles (4,610.8 km) of streams. Living in this majestic landscape are 71 mammal species, from the pygmy shrew—which weighs no more than a dime—to 500-pound (226.8 kg) elk. There are also 276 documented species of birds, 18 native fish species, and 1,990 plant species. The Blackfeet believe that all this land and the creatures living in it are sacred, but

SIZE OF PARK: 1,583 square miles (4,099.9 sq km) ★ **BEST TIME TO GO:** Year-round
YEAR ESTABLISHED: 1910 ★ **IN-PARK ACCOMMODATIONS:** Lodges & camping

Bowman Lake is the third largest lake in the park, after Lake McDonald and Saint Mary Lake.

In 2017, a group of park archaeologists, along with members of the Blackfeet Youth Corps, found more than 20 trees that had been "culturally modified," cut or scarred by humans. The modification comes in many forms: The outer bark of some ponderosa pines has been peeled to access the inner cambium layer, an important food source for Native Americans in the region. Other trees were scarred and marked over the years by rangers on patrol.

there is particular power in Ninaistako, or "Chief Mountain." This imposing peak, which can be seen from 100 miles (160.9 km) away, is an important ceremonial and ritual site for the Blackfeet and is linked to many of their creation stories.

One feature of the park that has changed dramatically since the days of Lewis and Clark, however, is the number of its glaciers. In 1850, there were about 80 glaciers in what would become Glacier National Park. Between 1966 and 2015,

There are 734 miles (223.7 km) of hiking trails throughout the park.

A mountain goat pauses on a rock near Hidden Lake.

Take in the grandeur of Glacier National Park from the stunning Avalanche Lake, surrounded by sweeping mountain views.

> 66 The park ... is still the most intact remaining temperate ecosystem in North America, where all the predators that were here before European settlement still remain. 99

every named glacier in the park receded, some by more than 80 percent. In 2015, the last year with satellite imagery available, there were 26 named glaciers that met the size criteria of .03 square mile (0.1 sq km). Of those 26, some have shrunk too small to still be considered glaciers.

In 2003, a U.S. geological study indicated that the park's glaciers would be gone by 2020. The park erected signs warning its visitors, but thankfully, 2020 came and went, and the signs have since been removed. While the glaciers are drastically shrinking, they haven't yet disappeared. ■

LITTLE BIGHORN BATTLEFIELD NATIONAL MONUMENT

★ ★

This haunting memorial on the lonesome prairie of the Northern Great Plains in south-central Montana marks a sad chapter in U.S. history. It was established as a national cemetery in 1879 to honor the estimated 263 U.S. Cavalry men and Native scouts who lost their lives here. However, the monument has evolved to include a more comprehensive picture of the enormous loss for the Northern Plains tribes: An entire way of life for the Lakota and Northern Cheyenne was disappearing.

By the late 1800s, the world had dramatically shrunk for the Native tribes who hunted buffalo across the Great Plains. While the Lakota Sioux had won a victory over the United States under the leadership of Red Cloud and signed the Fort Laramie treaty in 1868, which created the Great Sioux Reservation, other leaders, led by Sitting Bull and Crazy Horse, refused to be corralled. In 1874, gold had been found in the Black Hills, and the government wanted to buy this portion of the reservation. The Lakota Sioux refused. These events mark the beginning of the Great Sioux War of 1876, a bloody year of skirmishes and battles, the most storied of which was the Battle of the Little Bighorn.

SIZE OF PARK: 1.2 square miles (3.1 sq km) ★ BEST TIME TO GO: Year-round
YEAR ESTABLISHED: 1879 ★ IN-PARK ACCOMMODATIONS: None

Little Bighorn marked the most decisive Native American victory in the long Plains Indian War.

Lt. Col. George Armstrong Custer was part of a three-pronged attack coordinated by the War Department. On June 25, 1876, Custer and the 640 men of the Seventh Cavalry entered the valley of the Little Bighorn, in which a camp of 8,000 Northern Cheyenne and Lakota Sioux had gathered on the banks of the Little Bighorn River a week earlier to find game and grass for their 20,000 horses. Custer had planned a surprise attack for dawn of June 26, but his Crow and Arikara scouts sensed that the camp had detected the regiment's presence. Instead, Custer divided his troops and ordered Maj. Marcus Reno and his 140-men battalion to cross the river and lead a direct attack.

"Soldiers came at us like a thunderbolt," recounted Sioux chief Low Dog of Reno's attack. The fighting was fierce and fast, but Reno's forces were eventually outnumbered by the estimated 1,500 to 1,800 warriors who pushed them back into

Custer National Cemetery marks the graves of known and unknown veterans, Native scouts, and Medal of Honor recipients.

An iron sculpture in the park depicts a scene from the Battle of Greasy Grass.

WHAT'S IN A NAME?

Crazy Horse, a leader of the Oglala Lakota Sioux Nation, played an instrumental role in defeating General Custer and his troops in the Battle of the Little Bighorn. As a child, he went by the name Curly Hair, because of his impressive tendrils, and later just Curly. After a brave battle against an enemy Arapaho tribe, Curly Hair's father, also named Crazy Horse, bestowed his own name to his son and took the name Waglúla, or Worm.

the surrounding ridges. Soon after, the warriors rushed the ridge, today known as Last Stand Hill, where Custer himself was fighting, killing the commander and roughly 210 soldiers. The victory for the tribes was short-lived. Within a year, the "hostiles," as the tribes were known, had surrendered, and the U.S. government took the Black Hills. Sitting Bull was the last holdout and surrendered in 1881 after returning from Canada. ■

GREAT BASIN NATIONAL PARK

★★★★★★★★★★★★★★★★★★★★★★★★★

Great Basin National Park on the far eastern edge of central Nevada is a fascinating microcosm of the Great Basin, a 209,162-square-mile (541,730 sq km) terminal watershed that sprawls across the western United States, covering most of Nevada, a good portion of Oregon and Utah, and parts of California, Idaho, and Wyoming. The park encompasses the subterranean depths of 40 caves and the 13,065-foot (3,982.2 m) summit of Wheeler Peak.

Scattered in high-altitude subalpine groves live the bristlecone pines, the world's longest-living non-clonal organism. The oldest, the Prometheus tree, was estimated to have lived at least 4,862 years before a graduate student cut it down for research purposes in 1964. To put that time frame into perspective, Prometheus was older than Egypt's Great Pyramid of Giza.

Legend has it that in the late 1800s, a rancher named Absalom Lehman was riding his horse across his property when the horse's hoof broke through a crust that covered the entrance to a spectacular cavern. The cave had been known to Indigenous peoples perhaps as early as A.D. 1000 based on evidence of human bones discovered near its entrance. But Lehman named it after himself and spread the word, and it became an almost overnight sensation. Excited onlookers came from miles around to shine candlelit torches toward the stalactites, stalagmites, columns, and

SIZE OF PARK: 121 square miles (313 sq km) ★ **BEST TIME TO GO:** Year-round
YEAR ESTABLISHED: 1986 ★ **IN-PARK ACCOMMODATIONS:** Camping

Wheeler Peak stands above the park at 13,065 feet (3,982.2 m).

ECOLOGICAL HIGHLIGHT

Bristlecone pines are the longest-living tree. The secret to their longevity is that they grow in such harsh, cold, windy conditions above the tree line that some years bristlecones don't even add a full growth ring. As a result, the tree's wood is so dense that it is resistant to rot, fungi, insect infestation, and erosion.

other whimsical formations they found. Unfortunately, portions of the formations, some of which grow only four inches (10.2 cm) per century, were sold as souvenirs. The cave is still a confoundingly beautiful underworld, especially now that Fat Man's Misery—a passageway that required belly crawling—is no longer necessary to reach the Grand Palace, the crown jewel of the cave.

For sweeping park views, summit Wheeler Peak, the second highest peak in all of Nevada.

Tom turkeys run wild throughout the park, seen here in breeding plumage.

There are three bristlecone pine tree groves in the park, all of which sit right below the tree line at roughly 9,000 feet (2,743.2 m) above sea level. The easiest way to see these gnarled trees that have been twisted by wind, water, snow, and time is to hike 1.5 miles (2.4 km) up from the Wheeler Peak campground to the northeast-facing grove, where a self-guided nature trail passes through a portion of the trees, discernible by their needles, which grow in one-inch-long (2.5 cm) packets of five. These needles surround the branches in tightly bunched tufts. Don't be tempted to bring any of the downed wood home as a souvenir—it may be 1,000 years old. ■

66 The cave is still a confoundingly beautiful underworld. 99

CARLSBAD CAVERNS NATIONAL PARK

★ ★

To explore Carlsbad Caverns is to descend into deep time. Roughly 265 million years ago, this region of the Southwest was covered in the shallow Permian Sea, where calcareous sponges, algae, and lime-rich mud formed an enormous underwater fossil reef. The reef ultimately became a horseshoe-shaped limestone rock formation that stretched 400 miles (643.7 km) across what is now Texas and New Mexico.

Over the last 20 million years, faulting and uplift forced the reef 10,000 feet (3,048 m) upward. Between four and six million years ago, hydrogen-sulfide-rich underground water migrated through the faults in the limestone. When it mixed with rainwater falling from above, the two waters created sulfuric acid. This sulfuric acid dissolved the limestone to create what is now Carlsbad Caverns.

Of the 120 known caves within the national park, Lechuguilla, which is off-limits to the public, is the longest, stretching 145 miles (233 km) long and 1,604 feet (489 m) deep. In 1986, speleologists hit pay dirt when, following up on a rumor that air had seeped up from the cave floor, they dug through the bottom and found a large passageway. Today, Lechuguilla is one of the 10 longest caves in the world. Thirty-mile-long (48 km) Carlsbad Cavern, which is open to the public, contains the 8.2-acre (3.3 ha) Big Room, the largest cave chamber by volume in North America, which comedian Will Rogers once described as "the Grand Canyon with a roof over it." ■

SIZE OF PARK: 73.07 square miles (189.25 sq km) ★ **BEST TIME TO GO:** Year-round
YEAR ESTABLISHED: 1930 ★ **IN-PARK ACCOMMODATIONS:** Primitive camping

Gypsum chandeliers
descend from the ceiling
of Lechuguilla Cave.

WHITE SANDS NATIONAL PARK

★★★★★★★★★★★★★★★★★★★★★★★★★

This otherworldly stretch of the world's largest gypsum sand dunes is one of the United States' newest national parks. At first glance, one may wonder what can survive in this seemingly desolate swath of shifting sand. Upon closer inspection, however, its Chihuahuan Desert ecosystem, the most diverse in the Western Hemisphere, sustains more than 220 species of birds (great horned owl, red-tailed hawk, and greater roadrunner), an exotic host of reptiles (bleached earless lizard and endemic pale-blue little white whiptail), and elusive nocturnal mammals like the bobcat.

In the late 1960s, the New Mexico Department of Game and Fish introduced the African oryx at nearby White Sands Missile Range to entice hunters. Today the gemsbuck is banned from the park because it is detrimental to native fauna, but visitors occasionally catch a glimpse of one in the park, furthering its essence as an exotic landscape.

Mammals much larger than oryx have been roaming these parts since the Ice Age. In 2018, paleontologists discovered a "trackway" of more than 100 human footprints overlaid on prints determined to be that of a razor-clawed giant sloth about eight feet (2.4 m) in height. The pattern of the tracks indicates the sloth was on its

---

SIZE OF PARK: 230 square miles (595 sq km) ★ **BEST TIME TO GO:** Fall
YEAR ESTABLISHED: 2019 ★ **IN-PARK ACCOMMODATIONS:** Camping

Leave only footprints on your exploration of the white-sand dunes of New Mexico's national park.

hind legs, flailing at its human attackers. More human prints found in the distance indicate that the entire community took part in hunting the giant sloths. This impressive find marks the largest concentration of Ice Age mega-fauna fossilized footprints in the world.

To understand the alchemy of the dunes, take a ranger-guided hike to Lake Lucero between

The dunes at the park offer myriad options for recreation, including sand sledding and surfing.

Soapweed yucca bloom from the white sands throughout the park.

October and March. It's here in this dry lake bed where the wind-deposited gypsum precipitates into crystals of impure brown selenite found on the mudflats of the lakeshore. These crystals eventually erode into sand grains that ultimately shift into the towering dunes.

As anyone who has spent time in New Mexico can attest, sunsets in "the Land of Enchantment" are the most magical part of the day. At White Sands, the pastel pink, orange, and red hues of the sinking orb reflect on the dunes, exponentially amplifying the colors. For an even more ethereal evening, time your visit with the rise of a full moon. ■

“ Sunsets in 'the Land of Enchantment' are the most magical part of the day. ”

GILA WILDERNESS

★★★★★★★★★★★★★★★★★★★★★★★★

I n 1909, famed author and early ecologist Aldo Leopold, then a recent graduate of Yale, was working as a forester in Arizona. One day while eating lunch on a high rock above a river, Leopold and his companions saw a female wolf crossing the turbulent water. As was the practice at the time, the men shot at the wolf, an animal considered to be an aggressive predator. The animal dropped, and as Leopold recounted in *A Sand County Almanac,* "We reached the old wolf in time to watch a fierce green fire dying in her eyes."

That moment planted a seed that formed Leopold's now famous conservation philosophy, a world in which man was just one part of a greater community of interdependent parts. Everything in the landscape, the soil, water, plants, animals, and humans were all one. That philosophy has existed for millennia within Indigenous communities, but it was a revolutionary concept for an Anglo man in Leopold's position at the time. Using this "Land Ethic" as his guiding principle, Leopold proposed that the Forest Service should set aside more than 500,000 acres (202,342.8 ha) of mountains, rivers, and desert surrounding the Gila River in southwest New Mexico and designate it as wilderness—a landscape that should be left to its own devices. In 1924, the Gila became the first congressionally designated wilderness in the country.

This "wilderness," however, has been home to humans for more than 10,000 years—first to the Paleo-Indians who inhabited the region between 9,500 and 6,000 years ago, later to the Mogollon

SIZE OF PARK: 872 square miles (2,258 sq km) ★ **BEST TIME TO GO:** Year-round
YEAR ESTABLISHED: 1924 ★ **IN-PARK ACCOMMODATIONS:** Camping

Gila Cliff Dwellings, built along the canyon's natural caves, date back thousands of years.

Within the wilderness, near the headwaters of the Gila River, lie the Gila Cliff Dwellings, a 533-acre (215.6 hectare) settlement built by the Mogollon culture around 1280. The inhabitants, who lived there for about 20 years before moving on, farmed and hunted wild game, and were skilled potters. The remains of the dwellings lay undiscovered for centuries. Six years after the first recorded visit in 1878, the site was pillaged.

culture who built cliff dwellings here around A.D. 1280, and finally to the nomadic Apache who hunted and gathered in the Gila in the 16th and 17th centuries. Today's visitors can see it largely as it was in the day of Leopold. With hundreds of miles of trails accessible from 50 designated trailheads, hikers and horseback riders can traverse this hard-to-navigate country where many ecosystems converge: the 10,000-foot-plus (3,048 m) peaks of the Mogollon Mountains; Chihuahuan and Sonoran

Protected within Gila National Forest, the Mogollon Mountains stretch across southwestern New Mexico.

Peer into the cliff dwellings that border park trails.

Look for western black-necked garter snakes throughout the park.

> 66 Everything in the landscape, the soil, water, plants, animals, and humans were all one. 99

Desert landscape; and the West, Middle, and East Forks of the Gila River. Stretching more than 30 miles (48.3 km) each, these three rivers are the longest free-flowing waterways in New Mexico.

This intact ecosystem sustains abundant wildlife, including wild turkeys, pronghorn, elk, bighorn sheep, javelina, cougars, and black bears. Endangered Mexican wolves have been successfully reintroduced to the wilderness and have multiplied. The wilderness is also home to the world's largest population of rare Mexican spotted owls. ■

CRATER LAKE NATIONAL PARK

★★★★★★★★★★★★★★★★★★★★★★★★★

The Makalak people lived for thousands of years southeast of what is now Crater Lake National Park. Legends of how North America's deepest lake formed have been passed down to their descendants, the Klamath, for generations. The oral history of two powerful deities, Llao—the spirit of the mountain—and Skell—the spirit of the sky—is one of many that are still relevant to the Klamath today. As it goes:

One day as Llao stood atop Mount Mazama, he gazed upon the Makalak chief's beautiful daughter and fell in love with her. When she refused his advances, Llao became so angry that he decided to destroy her people with fire. Llao hurled red rocks, causing the earth to tremble, and created massive landslides, to which Skell responded with the same fury. To stop the fighting, two Makalak holy men jumped into the fiery pit on top of the mountain. Moved by their sacrifice, Skell drove Llao deep into the mountain.

The next morning, the peak was gone and a water-filled crater remained. From that day forward, the Makalak would not gaze into Crater Lake, believing to do so would cause death.

The resulting crater is still beautifully mysterious: Plunging to a depth of 1,943 feet (592 m), making it the deepest lake in the United States, and surrounded by 2,000-foot (609 m) sheer rock walls, the lake formed 7,700 years ago when 12,000-foot (3,657 m) Mount Mazama collapsed after a massive volcanic eruption.

SIZE OF PARK: 286.3 square miles (741.5 sq km) ★ **BEST TIME TO GO:** June to October
YEAR ESTABLISHED: 1902 ★ **IN-PARK ACCOMMODATIONS:** Lodges & camping

Crater Lake, formed 7,700 years ago, appears even more majestic during a winter's sunset.

The cerulean water that fills the crater is so clear that light has penetrated it to a depth of 142 feet (43 m). It's the only lake in the world inhabited by the Mazama newt, a salamander that scientists believed colonized the crater 6,000 years ago. Thick green bryophyte moss grows in a continuous ring around the caldera, and rising up out of the west side of the lake, like

Trails offer scenic opportunities to hike around the lake.

A golden-mantled ground squirrel stops to enjoy a nut.

Lush green forests border the majestic lake.

a backdrop from *Lord of the Rings*, is Wizard Island, the strikingly precipitous 767-foot-tall (233 m) remains of a cinder cone.

The largest mystery that remains, however, is where the water from the lake drains. The lake has no outlets, yet it receives an average of 528 inches (1,341 cm) of snowfall per year. Scientists now understand that roughly two million gallons of water an hour seep out of the caldera walls, but they still aren't certain where it all goes. No creeks, springs, or other nearby water sources have been found to contain the same water chemistry as Crater Lake. ∎

❝ The lake formed 7,700 years ago when … Mount Mazama collapsed after a massive volcanic eruption. ❞

ARCHES NATIONAL PARK

★★★★★★★★★★★★★★★★★★★★★★★★★

There are more than 2,000 rock arches in Arches National Park—the greatest concentration of these geologic structures in the world. This fascinating array of arches, which sit in the high desert of the Colorado Plateau at an elevation between 4,085 and 5,653 feet (1,361.7–1,884.3 m), is largely due to three powerful forces: time, water, and, most important, salt in the form of domes buried deep beneath overlying rock.

How these arches formed is a complicated geologic story that begins 300 million years ago. At that time, the region was a vast shallow embayment of an ocean to the west. The climate was hot and dry, and as the basin subsided, evaporated salt deposits accumulated to depths in excess of 10,000 feet (3,048 m). Over millennia, other sediments covered the salt deposits. Those in turn were buried and eventually transformed into rock. As time passed and geologic forces wrinkled, folded, and warped the rock, the deeply buried, less dense, and more plastic salt started migrating upward along zones of weakness in the overlying rock formations, eventually creating huge salt domes covered by a relatively thin veneer of sedimentary rock.

As the entire region began to rise, climbing from sea level to thousands of feet in elevation, erosion carved layer after layer of rock away. Once exposed, the deeply buried layers of sandstone directly above the salt deposits warped and expanded, creating even more

---

SIZE OF PARK: 120 square miles (310 sq km) ★ **BEST TIME TO GO:** Year-round
YEAR ESTABLISHED: 1971 ★ **IN-PARK ACCOMMODATIONS:** Camping

Spy the Turret Arch through the North Window at Arches National Park.

fractures, allowing for water—whether in the form of rain or snowmelt—to percolate down through the fissures and, critically, dissolve the upper portions of the salt domes. As the salt dome slowly collapsed, water eroded the overlying rock into long narrow fins perfect for arch formation. Continued percolation of water through the fins resulted in formation of the arches seen today.

Find Ute petroglyphs along the delicate arch hiking trail.

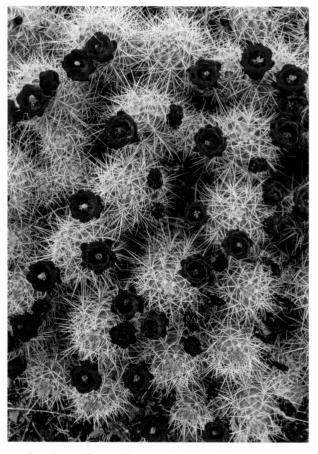

Stunning red flowers bloom on the limbs of claret cup cacti.

Arches National Park is known for more than 2,000 natural sandstone structures, as well as desert landscape.

It would take years to locate all 2,000 arches in the park, but the most iconic formations, like Double Arch, the tallest arch in the park at 112 feet (34 m), and Delicate Arch, the most famous natural rock structure in the world, are within easy view from pull offs along the park's main road. For the fewer than one percent of park visitors who choose to backcountry camp (at designated sites only), remember that the park contains delicate high-desert ecosystems, irreplaceable cultural resources, and limited water. ■

66 How these arches formed is a complicated geologic story that begins 300 million years ago. 99

BRYCE CANYON NATIONAL PARK

★ ★

Bryce Canyon, a series of 14 hoodoo-filled amphitheaters of deep red dolomitic limestone, is technically not a canyon. For a canyon to form, there needs to be a river—and the closest river to Bryce is the Paria, which flows five to 10 miles (8–16.1 km) east of the park. So how did the deep depressions of Bryce form?

The short answer is that between 50 and 30 million years ago, rocks were deposited in an ancient freshwater lake basin. Twenty million years of continuous deposits followed by tectonic uplift of the Colorado Plateau region created the Paunsaugunt Plateau, on which 8,000-foot (2,438.4 m) Bryce now sits.

The natural forces at this elevation, including rain, wind, melting snow, gravity, and, most important, frost, started irregularly eroding the rock bed, creating the park's thousands of spires known as hoodoos.

These mystical hoodoos are what most of the 2.6 million annual visitors come to see, hiking trails like the 1.3-mile (2.1 km) Navajo Loop, which descends into Bryce amphitheater through a slot canyon lined by Douglas fir trees. But Bryce also has two rugged backcountry hiking trail options, the 23-mile (37 km) Under the Rim Trail and the nine-mile (14.5 km) Riggs Spring Loop, both of which meander through alpine forests with distant views to multihued buttes and cliffs. The lesser-traveled backcountry is an excellent way to observe the park's smaller beauties, like

SIZE OF PARK: 55.9 square miles (144.7 sq km) ★ **BEST TIME TO GO:** Year-round
YEAR ESTABLISHED: 1928 ★ **IN-PARK ACCOMMODATIONS:** Lodges & camping

Take to the skies in a hot-air balloon for another perspective of Bryce's majesty.

wildflower-laced meadows and the Utah prairie dog, a once endangered species that was expected to go extinct by 2000. Thanks to the park's efforts, the prairie dog is now bouncing back and plays an essential role in maintaining its grassland ecology. Another excellent way to avoid the April-to-October high-season traffic is to cycle the 17-mile (27.4 km) bike path that connects the park

Snow covers the mountains and hoodoos of Bryce come winter, a great time to visit to avoid the crowds.

A ponderosa pine perches on the edge of a cliff in the park.

Take a horseback ride along the park's Hoodoo Trail.

> **"** Bryce's stark beauty shines in the winter, when there are fewer visitors and the bright white snow glistens against the deep red rock. **"**

to Red Canyon, a lesser-known hoodoo-filled depression on the other side of the plateau.

One might assume the best time to visit this park is in the height of summer, but Bryce's stark beauty shines in the winter, when there are fewer visitors and the bright white snow glistens against the deep red rock. It's the ideal time to take a ranger-led snowshoe tour of the canyon rim or head off into the backcountry on skis. Because the sky is so unaffected by light pollution, Bryce is one of the only places in the country where the Milky Way is visible in the winter. ■

CAPITOL REEF NATIONAL PARK

★ ★

Before Capitol Reef was designated as a national park, its wild rock formations were known to those nearby as Wayne Wonderland. The name was fitting. Partially located in Wayne County, Utah, the region contained otherworldly cliffs, spires, and buttes that wowed the few intrepid souls who explored the rugged country.

The foundation for these formations is the 100-mile-long (160.9 km) Waterpocket Fold. This classic monocline is a warp in Earth's crust that formed 50 million to 70 million years ago when movement along a deeply buried fault caused the rock formations west of the fault to shift more than 7,000 feet (2,134 m) higher than the same formations east of the fault. Erosion exposed this giant step up in the landscape 20 million to 15 million years ago. Over subsequent millennia, water eroded the rock into its current formations, including the white Navajo Sandstone domes for which the park is named because they are reminiscent of the rotunda on the U.S. Capitol building.

Because it was primarily designated to protect the Waterpocket Fold, the park is a skinny rectangle. In the southern Waterpocket District, a short 0.4-mile (0.6 km) hike to the Strike Valley Overlook takes visitors to an expansive view of almost a dozen clearly striated sedimentary rock layers that represent more than 150 million years of geologic history. In the park's remote northern Cathedral Valley district, sandstone fins, reminiscent of Gothic cathedrals, jut into the sky. ∎

SIZE OF PARK: 378 square miles (979 sq km) ★ **BEST TIME TO GO:** Year-round
YEAR ESTABLISHED: 1971 ★ **IN-PARK ACCOMMODATIONS:** Camping

The historic Fruita Barn sits in front of the red mountains of Capitol Reef.

CANYONLANDS NATIONAL PARK

★★★★★★★★★★★★★★★★★★★★★★★★★

This arid, isolated region of fantastical rock formations appears to be a no-man's-land of nearly impenetrable red-canyon mazes, carved by the Colorado and Green Rivers. But humans have been migrating through and living in what is now Canyonlands National Park for 10,000 years, first to make seasonal rounds hunting game and gathering wild plants, and later to settle and farm, like the ancestral Puebloans did successfully as recently as 700 years ago until they were driven out by consistent drought. In the 1800s, robbers like Butch Cassidy found its puzzling rock mazes a convenient place to hide out.

Modern-day hikers, climbers, horseback riders, and campers have the Cold War to thank for the relative ease with which they can now access Canyonlands National Park. In the 1950s, the Atomic Energy Commission believed this area to be rich in uranium, a critical ingredient in nuclear weapons. To find it, they hired a small army of prospectors who built almost 1,000 miles (1,600 km) of roads in southeastern Utah, many of which are in what is now the national park. These roads, built with bulldozers and the back-breaking labor of picks and shovels, forever altered Canyonlands with very little return on the investment. The prospectors found almost

SIZE OF PARK: 527 square miles (1,366.2 sq km) ★ BEST TIME TO GO: Year-round
YEAR ESTABLISHED: 1964 ★ IN-PARK ACCOMMODATIONS: Camping

Chesler Park winds through stunning sandstone pinnacles, knobs, and fins in the Needles district of the park.

no uranium within the boundaries of the park, but their roads opened up this nearly inaccessible region to hordes of visitors.

Dissected by the Colorado and Green Rivers, which converge in Canyonlands, the park is naturally split into three main sections—Island in the Sky, the Needles, and the Maze—none of which are accessible to the other, unless visitors happen to be floating through the park on one of the two rivers. Of the three, Island in the Sky and Needles

Take your mountain bike for a spin on the White Rim trail along Monument Basin.

Discover ancient Native American petroglyphs at Newspaper Rock.

Camp in view of the rocky mesas from your tent.

are the most accessible, with paved park roads that offer many pullouts for spectacular views of the mesas, buttes, and arches. The Maze offers the most rugged and remote wilderness, with no paved roads.

One of the most fascinating areas of the park is the detached Horseshoe Canyon section. This contains the Great Gallery, a 200-foot-long (61 m) by 15-foot-high (4.6 m) panel of 20 life-size pictographs and petroglyphs. These figures represent one of the largest and best preserved collections of rock markings in North America. To reach the Great Gallery requires a rugged, seven-mile (11.3 km) round-trip hike that climbs 750 feet (228.6 m). But the haunting display of Late Archaic work is worth every step. ▪

66 The park is naturally split into three main sections— Island in the Sky, the Needles, and the Maze. 99

ZION NATIONAL PARK

★ ★

U tah's first national park is perhaps its most dramatic. Walking below 2,000-foot-high (609.6 m), coral-colored sandstone cliffs is like inhabiting an alternate universe, one in which time stands still. In a way, time has stood still in Zion—the names of its most iconic formations and structures are each rooted in a particular moment in history.

The Virgin River was so named by Spanish Catholic missionaries in the 1700s. Zion is an ancient Hebrew word meaning "sanctuary" that Mormon settlers bestowed upon this magical place in the 1850s. Mukuntuweap is a Paiute word meaning "straight canyon" that Maj. John Wesley Powell bestowed upon what is now Zion Canyon on a surveying expedition in 1872 to honor the people who have lived here for centuries.

The southern Paiute still refer to the park's centerpiece as Mukuntuweap. Carved by the Virgin River 250 million years ago, the chasm is 15 miles (24.1 km) long and a half mile (0.8 km) deep in some places. The Narrows, surveyed by Powell's expedition, is the slimmest section of the gorge. Here the river stretches only 20 feet (6.1 m) across with canyon walls that shoot 2,000 feet (609.6 m) into the sky on either side. Angels Landing, a rocky promontory 1,000 feet (304.8 m) above the river has sheer drop-offs on either side and views to canyons in every direction.

The original Zion Lodge, which sat at the base of the canyon, was one of the most intimate and understated of all the iconic national park lodges. The original 1925 lodge, designed by Gilbert Stanley Underwood, the Yale- and Harvard-educated architect who also designed Yosemite's Ahwahnee lodge, was a labor of love. Workers had to winch 265,000 board feet (80,772 m) of lumber 2,000 vertical feet (609.6 m)

SIZE OF PARK: 229 square miles (593.1 sq km) ★ **BEST TIME TO GO:** Year-round
YEAR ESTABLISHED: 1919 ★ **IN-PARK ACCOMMODATIONS:** Lodges & camping

Seek adrenaline-rushing thrills—like rappelling down cliffs—in Zion.

into the canyon from the plateau above using the Cable Mountain Draw Works, a wire-and-pulley tramway, parts of which are still visible today. The original lodge burned to the ground in 1966. To keep guests happy, the Utah Parks Company built a new prefabricated lodge structure that was up and running in less than four months, but it had little of the understated elegance of its predecessor.

Walter's Wiggles begins the 1.8-mile (2.9 km) hike to Angels Landing.

Spot bighorn rams standing on sandstone cliffs throughout the park.

Take Highway 9 through Zion to see some of the park's most iconic landmarks and to access Zion Canyon.

> ❝ Walking below ... sandstone cliffs is like inhabiting an alternate universe, one in which time stands still. ❞

Every year, increasing numbers of visitors flock to Zion. The park now averages 4.5 million visitors annually. With its increasing popularity, especially in such highly concentrated areas, it's essential that visitors respect this place that is so sacred to the Paiute: Plan ahead, stay away from canyons during flash flooding, hike on established trails only, practice leave-no-trace wilderness ethics, and protect the canyon walls from graffiti and vandalism. ■

MOUNT RAINIER NATIONAL PARK

★★★★★★★★★★★★★★★★★★★★★★★

Mount Rainier, an active volcano and the most glaciated summit in the lower 48, has captivated imaginations for millennia, whether it be those of the region's six original affiliated tribes—the Nisqually, Puyallup, Squaxin Island, Muckleshoot, Yakama, and Cowlitz—who continue to hunt and gather plants on the land, the mountaineers who first reached the summit in 1870, or naturalists like John Muir, who after his 1888 ascent proclaimed that the peak's flanks contained "the most luxuriant and the most extravagantly beautiful of all the alpine gardens I ever beheld in all my mountain-top wanderings."

The country's fifth-oldest national park has played an especially critical role as a proving ground for mountaineers, a tradition that began 150 years ago when writer P. B. Van Trump and his friend General Hazard Stevens made the first recorded ascent of the 14,410-foot (4,392.2 m) peak in 1870. Unprepared for the cold, the two had to spend the night in the summit crater huddled in a cavern warmed by sulfurous steam. A decade later, Fay Fuller, wearing woolen hosiery, a thick wool bloomer suit, and boys' calfskin shoes with caulks, became the first woman to summit the peak at age 20.

By 1905, the only two official mountaineering groups in the west—San Francisco's Sierra Club and

SIZE OF PARK: 369.3 square miles (956.4 sq km) ★ **BEST TIME TO GO:** June & October
YEAR ESTABLISHED: 1899 ★ **IN-PARK ACCOMMODATIONS:** Lodges & camping

Wildflowers bloom in the grassy meadows at the foot of snowcapped Mount Rainier.

BOTANY 101

Mount Rainier is ringed by subalpine meadows that are full of hundreds of species of wildflowers, including alpine asters, glacier lilies, cascade huckleberries, and scarlet paintbrush. Because the mountain receives so much snow in the winter, the flowers' growing season is extremely short and the plants need to expend their energy on rapid flowering. The reduced time frame leaves them few resources to fight damage from, say, being trampled, the reason it is essential that park visitors remain on trails while hiking.

Portland's Mazamas (which Fuller helped found)—began organizing expeditions to Rainier. Camped side by side at an area known as Paradise Park at 5,400 feet (1,645.9 m) on the peak's south slope, the groups—comprising both men and women—would listen to campfire chats by scientists and professors, afterward playing pranks on each other under the cover of night. In 1906, a third group, the Mountaineers, formed in Seattle and became instrumental in shaping future park policy. One of its future members, Jim Whittaker,

With mountaineering experience, you can take on the challenge of summiting Rainier, which stands at 14,410 feet (4,392.2 m).

Stop in at the visitors center at the aptly named Paradise.

Christine Falls Bridge spans the lower portion of the cascade.

became the first American to summit Mount Everest in 1963.

A fraction of park visitors, however, go to the top. The park's 93-mile-long (149.7 km) Wonderland Trail is a striking alternative, circumnavigating rather than summiting Mount Rainier. This epic meander takes hikers through some of the most beautiful terrain in the Pacific Northwest, from wildflower-filled subalpine meadows over rivers and streams to wide-open valleys with unobstructed views of the glaciated peak. With 18 designated wilderness camps and four resupply mailboxes along the way, the trail is ideal for backcountry hikers who want to go long. ■

66 The park's … Wonderland Trail is a striking alternative, circumnavigating rather than summiting Mount Rainier. 99

NORTH CASCADES NATIONAL PARK

★★★★★★★★★★★★★★★★★★★★★★★★★

North Cascades sits only three hours east of the nearly four million people who live in the Seattle metro area, yet it is one of the least visited and least accessible national parks in the United States. There's good reason for that: The park is buffered on all sides by wilderness, national forest, or Canadian provincial parks.

Further, Ross Lake National Recreation Area splits the park in two and is the corridor for State Route 20, the only paved road accessing the greater park complex, which at 1,070 square miles (2,771 sq km) also includes Lake Chelan National Recreation Area directly south of the park.

It may be difficult to access, but North Cascades National Park is an alpine wonderland of jagged granite peaks, the highest of which, Goode Mountain, stretches 9,206 feet (2,805 m) into the sky; isolated groves of old-growth western red cedar that have escaped the fate of the saw blade;

and both frozen and fresh water—almost 300 glaciers sit within park boundaries, in addition to mountain-lined turquoise lakes, hundreds of streams cascading down precipitous mountainsides, and major rivers like the Skagit, which contains all five species of Pacific salmon. With all this water in which to fish, paddle, and float; more than 400 miles (643.7 km) of trails to hike; and seemingly endless mountains to climb, the park provides lifetimes of opportunity to explore an intact ecosystem, a feature that has almost ceased to exist in the lower 48. ■

SIZE OF PARK: 789 square miles (2,043 sq km) ★ **BEST TIME TO GO:** June to September
YEAR ESTABLISHED: 1968 ★ **IN-PARK ACCOMMODATIONS:** Lodges & camping

There are more than 400 miles (643.7 km) of trails to explore throughout the park.

OLYMPIC NATIONAL PARK

★★★★★★★★★★★★★★★★★★★★★★★★★★

Covering almost one million acres (404,685.6 ha), Washington's Olympic National Park sprawls across the Olympic Peninsula, which is bounded on the west by the Pacific Ocean, the north by the Strait of Juan de Fuca, and the east by Hood Canal. The park is only 36 miles (57.9 km) west of Seattle, but it immediately conjures images of misty primeval, moss-covered rainforests. Receiving more than 12 to 14 feet (3.7–4.3 m) of rain per year, it's no wonder these lush, protected forests in the Quinault, Queets, Hoh, and Bogachiel valleys are some of the best examples of temperate rainforest left in the United States.

But these forests are only a fraction of Olympic's spectacular diversity: The park also holds glacier-capped peaks, backcountry thermal hot springs, and a remote Pacific shoreline teeming with tide-pool life.

This rich diversity has served humans well over thousands of years. In 1977, a farmer named Emanuel Manis was digging on his property just outside the park when he unearthed a mastodon tusk. Archaeologists later found a spear point embedded in the rib bone of the 14,991-pound (6,800 kg) fossil. They determined that the spear didn't kill the mastodon, but the important finding marks the earliest known evidence of

SIZE OF PARK: 1,442 square miles (3,734.7 sq km) ★ BEST TIME TO GO: Year-round
YEAR ESTABLISHED: 1938 ★ IN-PARK ACCOMMODATIONS: Lodges & camping

Pitch your tent on Oregon's wild coast within Olympic National Park.

interaction between humans and mastodons in the Americas. Subsequent excavating revealed evidence of at least 12 levels of human occupation ranging from nearly 14,000 to 7,000 years ago. In the park itself, there are more than 650 archaeological sites that document 12,000 years of human occupation. The Makah Tribe, skilled mariners and fishermen whose history in the

Trails throughout Olympic National Park take you above the clouds, offering epic natural views.

Look up to the limbs to spot barred owls roosting in the trees.

A field of lupines blooms within the park's vast acreage.

park dates back 3,800 years, still inhabits the Olympic Peninsula.

Most people visit in summer, when they can hike Olympic's more than 600 miles (965.6 km) of trails, like the 18.2 mile (29.3 km) High Divide Loop that offers views to 9,573-foot (2,917.9 m) Mount Olympus; tide-pool for fish, plants, and invertebrates along the park's 70 miles (112.7 km) of Pacific Coastline; or hike through a forested cathedral. But there are also advantages to visiting in winter. Olympic has one of the few lift-served ski areas in a national park. This family-friendly resort that sits at 5,200 feet (1,585 m) along Hurricane Ridge has a chalet, two rope tows, a Poma lift, and a tubing hill offering skiers, snowboarders, and tubers a snowy wonderland with spectacular 360-degree views. ■

66 It's no wonder these lush, protected forests ... are some of the best examples of temperate rainforest left in the United States. 99

GRAND TETON NATIONAL PARK

★★★★★★★★★★★★★★★★★★★★★★★★★

Perhaps the most searing image of the Rocky Mountain American West is the jagged Teton Range, with majestic 13,770-foot (4,197.1 m) Grand Teton jutting from Jackson Hole, the 55-mile-long (88.5 km) valley through which the Snake River flows. This rugged landscape has been a place of spiritual sustenance and abundance for 23 Native American tribes since the nomadic Paleo-Indians came to the valley when glaciers began retreating 11,000 years ago.

For centuries, Shoshone, Bannock, Blackfeet, Crow, Flathead, Gros Ventre, Nez Perce, and other tribes have harvested roots and berries, fished for trout, and hunted the big game like bison, moose, and elk, all of which are still plentiful here.

The jaw-dropping beauty of the Tetons wasn't lost on European fur trappers and explorers, and, later, homesteaders and ranchers, who began to settle the area. At Mormon Row, which sits in the valley under the shadow of Blacktail Butte, there's a fascinating cluster of farms that were once home to several families of Mormon homesteaders who migrated here in the 1800s working together in a tightly knit community, hand-building a series of levees and dykes to irrigate their crops. The site offers visitors a glimpse of both the hardship of settling the West and the exhilaration of living in view of towering snow-capped peaks and herds of grazing bison.

SIZE OF PARK: 485 square miles (1,256 sq km) ★ **BEST TIME TO GO:** Year-round
YEAR ESTABLISHED: 1929 ★ **IN-PARK ACCOMMODATIONS:** Lodges & camping

Take in the massive Teton Range from the Snake River lookout.

In 1927, understanding the immense value of the region for the public, the philanthropist John D. Rockefeller, Jr., opened a shell business, the Snake River Land Company, to buy up parcels of land and donate them to the National Park Service in order to expand the forthcoming Teton National Park, which would protect only the high peaks. By 1930, word of his plan got out, and local landowners were furious at having been duped by the conservationist. The heated controversy lasted for more than a decade, until 1943, when President Franklin D. Roosevelt created the adjacent 221,000-acre (89,435.5 ha) Jackson Hole National Monument with land donated by the Snake River Land Company and additional acreage from Teton National Forest. In 1950, President Harry Truman signed a law that merged the national monument with Grand Teton National Park.

Rebounding from near extinction, close to 1,000 bison reside—and are protected—within Grand Teton National Park.

With a trophy like the Grand Teton surrounded by a spectacular alpine playground, it's no surprise that mountaineers, rock climbers, and skiers gravitate toward this mountain range. There is controversy around whether the two men—James Stevenson and Nathaniel Langford—who claimed to be the first to summit the peak in July 1872 actually made it to the top. But there is no question that the first woman, Eleanor Davis, a physical education teacher from Colorado College, reached the summit in 1923. A year later, Paul Petzoldt, a legendary mountaineer who would later found the National Outdoor Leadership School, became the youngest person to summit the Grand at age 16, a feat he allegedly accomplished while wearing cowboy boots.

One doesn't have to be a world class mountaineer to enjoy the stunning beauty of the park. But the hiking in the Tetons can be challenging—the terrain is precipitous, and there's often snow in the higher altitudes even in the middle of summer. The payoff is scenery that will forever be etched in your memory and a thriving abundance of wildlife, from bison, moose, and pronghorn

Backpack down Cascade Canyon on Mount Owen.

WILDLIFE SIGHTING

Grizzlies were almost decimated from the park's ecosystem nearly 40 years ago because of hunting and eradication programs. The bear, however, has made a fierce comeback thanks to concerted conservation efforts. The Greater Yellowstone Ecosystem, of which the park is a part, contains roughly 800 grizzlies.

grazing below a golden eagle in the valley to a chance encounter with a grizzly bear or mountain lion up high. Because the park is seeing increased visitation, it's a good idea to do your homework before visiting and make your way to the most popular sites, like Jenny Lake, a shimmering body of water below the peaks, at off times like sunrise or sunset, which also increases your odds of encountering wildlife. ■

Grand Teton is known
for its majestic mountain
scenery that includes
310,000 acres (125,452.5 ha).

PART TWO

OFF THE MAINLAND

The North Fork of the
Koyukuk River cuts through
Gates of the Arctic
National Park (p. 166).

LAKE CLARK NATIONAL PARK AND PRESERVE

★ ★

By Alaska standards, Lake Clark National Park is almost in Anchorage's backyard. The park—159 miles (255.9 km) to the southwest across Cook Inlet—is the size of Connecticut and Rhode Island combined and accessible only by boat or float plane. It sees roughly 23,000 visitors per year, less than half as many as Walt Disney World sees in a day. And most of its visitors are from Alaska.

The lucky few who get to see this under-the-radar wilderness, which sits at the nexus of the Alaska and Aleutian Ranges, experience a microcosm of the state's grandeur: an intact ecosystem of soaring active volcanoes that reach 10,000 feet (3,048 m), isolated salt marshes with salmon runs and clam beds that support one of the world's highest densities of brown bears, and lakes and rivers that are critical spawning habitats for sockeye salmon. (Lake Clark National Park sits at the headwaters of one of the largest sockeye salmon fisheries in the world.)

With all the fish, it's no wonder that the park supports a healthy population of brown bears. In May and early June, the bears congregate at the salt marshes along Cook Inlet to mate, dig for

SIZE OF PARK: 6,296 square miles (16,306 sq km) ★ **BEST TIME TO GO:** June to September
YEAR ESTABLISHED: 1980 ★ **IN-PARK ACCOMMODATIONS:** Lodges & camping

Beneath snowcapped peaks, Upper Twin Lake runs through Lake Clark National Park.

clams, and eat green sedges, a powerful and plentiful protein source. In one recent survey, park biologists counted 219 bears within a 54-square-mile (139.9 sq km) area along the coastline. As the sockeye and silver salmon return upriver to spawn, the bears are in hot pursuit. By August, Crescent Lake—a stunning turquoise body of water at the base of 10,197-foot (3,108 m) Mount Redoubt—is practically ringed by brown bears, which are competing with fishermen for the catch of a lifetime.

A brown bear looks up from its resting spot in the meadow near Silver Salmon Creek Lodge.

Because the resources are so abundant here, the largest males can weigh up to 1,000 pounds (453.6 kg) before returning to hibernation in the fall.

In addition to its intact natural ecosystem, the park still contains an intact cultural ecosystem as well. The ancestral homeland of the Dena'ina people, the region that is now the park contained four villages until about 200 years ago. One of them, Qizhjeh (Kijik Village), thrived on the shore of Qizhjeh Vena ("place where people gather lake"), which today is Lake Clark, a 40-mile-long (64.4 km) body of water draped by mountains. With strong salmon runs, abundant animals to hunt, and ample firewood, the community was a transportation hub, trading center, and important spiritual gathering place for almost a millennia, making it the longest year-round inhabited Indigenous village in Alaska. In the early 1900s, the residents were impacted by a flu-measles epidemic brought in by outsiders and surviving villagers moved the village down lake. Today the ancestral village site is a spruce forest surrounded by yawning wilderness, but every summer, the Dena'ina return to this sacred place to honor their ancestors. As part of

Lake Clark and the park's Twin Lakes offer miles of paddling.

that ritual, they have instituted a camp known as Quk' Taz'un, or "The Sun Is Rising," an opportunity for younger generations to learn the history and culture of their ancestors.

Because the park is within an hour's flight from Anchorage, it's an ideal place for visitors to immerse themselves quickly in rugged wilderness. There are several privately run lodges, but for those who have extensive bear-safety and camping experience, Lake Clark is a place to have a transformative wilderness adventure that starts the moment the air taxi lands. As the plane flies away, you too will be part of this spectacular wilderness that people have called home for centuries. ■

WILDLIFE SIGHTING

Every year, 372,000 sockeye salmon swim up the Newhalen River and enter the waters of the park, returning to the creeks, streams, and rivers where they were born. When the salmon start their migration, they develop an elongated snout with sharp teeth, which they use as a weapon against competing fish.

Wade into the streams throughout Lake Clark for excellent fly-fishing.

DENALI NATIONAL PARK AND PRESERVE

★★★★★★★★★★★★★★★★★★★★★★★★

Alaskan huskies are partially to thank for the existence of Denali National Park. In the winter of 1907-08, when naturalist Charles Sheldon needed a guide to navigate Denali country during his study of Dall sheep, he hired Alaskan dog musher Harry Karstens. Sheldon was so enamored with the experience and the surrounding wilderness that he returned home to the East Coast and successfully lobbied Congress to create a national park, which was officially designated in 1917.

The first park ranger was none other than Sheldon's guide, Harry Karstens. One of Karstens' first priorities was to create a park kennel in the interest of building teams of dogs to patrol the region throughout the winter for poachers who were decimating the caribou, moose, and Dall sheep populations. A century later, Denali's sled dogs still aid rangers in patrolling an average of 3,000 miles (4,828 km) throughout the park in winter.

The aboriginal homeland of five Northern Athabaskan groups—Dena'ina, Koyukon, Lower Tanana, Upper Kuskokwim, and Western Ahtna—Denali has diverse cultural heritage and a wealth of stories of early pioneers, like nurse and naturalist Fanny Quigley, who arrived in the Kantishna Hills during the gold rush and sent at least seven black bear specimens to the Smithsonian Institute for classification. In 1930, Count Ilya Tolstoy, the

SIZE OF PARK: 9,446 square miles (24,464 sq km) ★ **BEST TIME TO GO:** June to August
YEAR ESTABLISHED: 1917 ★ **IN-PARK ACCOMMODATIONS:** Lodges & camping

The sun rises over a frozen Otto Lake, beneath the snowy mountains of Denali.

The aurora borealis performs its green dance above the snowy peaks throughout Denali National Park.

WHAT'S IN A NAME?

Denali versus McKinley: Despite park advocates' efforts to name the park Denali in 1916, Thomas Riggs of the Alaska Engineering Commission overruled the request. It took almost a century to officially change the park's name from McKinley to Denali, which finally happened in 2015 under the Obama administration.

grandson of the great Russian novelist Leo Tolstoy, worked in the park for the summer. All of them were drawn here by the abundance of wildlife— Dall sheep, moose, bears, wolves, lynx, foxes, and more—and the spiritual majesty of 20,310-foot (6,190.5 m) Denali, which means "the Great One" in the Koyukon Athabaskan language. The third-most isolated peak on Earth, Denali is so massive that it floats like an apparition on the horizon. On a clear day, it can be seen from 200 miles (321.9 km) away.

With six million acres (2,428,113.8 ha) and only one road from which to explore it, the park has created an efficient and well-established shuttle system that has multiple options depending on how visitors want to see the park. Choose between free point-to-point shuttles, narrated bus tours with a park naturalist, or transit buses that, for those with a pass, can be hailed anywhere along the road to allow hikers and campers more flexibility. ■

> 66 Denali has diverse cultural heritage and a wealth of stories of early pioneers. 99

The Savage River cuts through a portion of the park.

There are nearly 1,800 caribou throughout Denali National Park.

GATES OF THE ARCTIC NATIONAL PARK AND PRESERVE

★★★★★★★★★★★★★★★★★★★★★★★★★

There are no roads, no signs, no designated campgrounds, and no trails in this vast wilderness that lies completely north of the Arctic Circle. But what Gates of the Arctic National Park and Preserve does contain are the 4,000-plus-foot (1,219.2 m) glaciated peaks of the Brooks Range, six Wild and Scenic Rivers, and three herds of migrating caribou that number in the hundreds of thousands.

The park also has the increasingly hard-to-find attributes of solitude and a sense of freedom that hasn't changed since famed forester, author, and conservationist Bob Marshall explored the central Brooks Range back in the 1930s.

The Nunamiut people still enjoy these attributes every day to survive this unforgiving landscape. In the late 1940s, these formerly coastal Eskimos were starving and had to move inland to find new areas to hunt and fish. Some settled in the village of Anaktuvuk Pass, the sole human settlement within the park. The estimated 250 residents here live largely as they have for centuries, hunting caribou, fishing for trout and grayling, and collecting firewood to keep them alive through the intense winters.

SIZE OF PARK: 13,238 square miles (34,286 sq km) ★ **BEST TIME TO GO:** Summer & fall
YEAR ESTABLISHED: 1980 ★ **IN-PARK ACCOMMODATIONS:** Camping

Sled dog team Wild and Free Mushing trots through the Brooks Range in Gates of the Arctic.

Of the 10,000 annual visitors to the park, many fly in via bush plane and are dropped off to float a river or hike out. (Impatient hikers take note: The

lack of trails, dense vegetation, boggy ground, and frequent stream and river crossings mean that a good day's hike is considered to be six miles/9.7 km.) While this amount of vast, unpopulated space can be liberating, it can also be a life-or-death test of self-reliance: Weather is unpredictable, help is far away, and guests share this space with wolves, grizzlies, and moose. It's essential to take backcountry and leave-no-trace orientations at the visitors centers in Fairbanks, Bettles, or

Make the trek along the shore of Arrigetch Creek, with Xanadu and Arial peaks as your views.

Mount Doonerak is partially obscured by beautiful blowing snow.

Find foliage like bearberry and caribou lichen throughout the park.

Coldfoot before entering the park; leave a back-country trip plan with park officials; and carry and store food in bear-resistant containers. Be well aware that communication within the park relies on spotty satellite service. If something should go wrong, the closest city, Fairbanks, is a 200-mile (321.9 km) bush flight south.

The rewards, however, outweigh the potential hazards. Whether photographing the migrating Western Arctic caribou herd, undertaking a 40-day expedition into the Brooks Range to rock climb the rugged granite spires of the Arrigetch Peaks, or floating under the snowcapped mountains that line the Wild and Scenic–designated Alatna River, this park leaves an indelible mark on every visitor's soul. ∎

66 The rewards, however, outweigh the potential hazards ... this park leaves an indelible mark on every visitor's soul. 99

WRANGELL–ST. ELIAS NATIONAL PARK

★★★★★★★★★★★★★★★★★★★★★★★★

For those who need a little space, there's no better place to find it than in the United States' largest national park. Six times larger than Yellowstone and 17 times larger than Yosemite, Wrangell–St. Elias contains four mountain ranges, a glacier that flows out of the St. Elias range in a mass that's larger than the state of Rhode Island, portions of the largest boreal forest ecosystem in the world, and miles and miles of flowing rivers. For all this space, there are only two dirt roads that stretch a combined 100 miles (160.9 km) into the park. It's no wonder most adventures here require a bush plane.

Such a vast, rugged expanse may seem hostile to human habitation, but archaeological evidence shows that hunter-gatherers began visiting the region northwest of the park 14,000 years ago. Four Alaska Native groups still live in and around the park. They are the Ahtna, Upper Tanana, Eyak, and Tlingit, who fish for salmon, hunt moose and caribou, and gather plants, berries, and mushrooms for food and medicine.

Adventurers will want to pore over a map before planning an adventure here because the possibilities are almost endless. With just a few days' time, visitors can charter a flight over the Wrangell Mountains; hike on the Root Glacier in Kennecott

SIZE OF PARK: 20,587.3 square miles (53,602 sq km) ★ **BEST TIME TO GO:** Summer
YEAR ESTABLISHED: 1980 ★ **IN-PARK ACCOMMODATIONS:** Lodges & camping

Take a bush plane tour above the glaciers of Wrangell–St. Elias.

to the Stairway Icefall, which cascades 6,000 feet (1,828.8 m) off of Mount Regal; hike 2.5 miles (4 km) up through the extinct, deeply eroded Skookum Volcano for an up-close look at volcanic geology; or drive to McCarthy, a laid-back historic mining town that's now the jumping-off point for white-water trips on multiple area rivers. Be sure to save an evening for a night of live music at the Golden Saloon in McCarthy.

Tour the historic buildings of the once bustling Kennecott Copper Mine.

Visit the park in the fall for milder weather and beautiful colors as the leaves turn for the season.

> 66 There are no maintained trails in the backcountry. The idea of wilderness, after all, is to be able to find your own way. 99

If a multi-day backpacking, packrafting, or climbing expedition is on the bucket list, note that there are no maintained trails in the backcountry. The idea of wilderness, after all, is to be able to find your own way. There are backcountry park rangers who can help plan a route in advance as well as 14 rugged huts—once used by miners, trappers, and hunters—accessible via remote airstrips. Though rustic, the cabins will ease the shock of being dropped off in the middle of the Alaskan bush. ■

GLACIER BAY NATIONAL PARK AND PRESERVE

★★★★★★★★★★★★★★★★★★★★★★★★★

Two hundred and fifty years ago, Glacier Bay, which sits 93 miles (149.7 km) west of Juneau, didn't exist. This region of southeast Alaska was under an enormous ice sheet. As the glacier started retreating in 1750, a magnificent abundance of flora and fauna started to grow and inhabit the space the glacier formerly occupied. In 1879, naturalist John Muir canoed up southeast Alaska's Inside Passage from Fort Wrangell to Glacier Bay, accompanied by three Tlingit guides.

On the first of four visits, Muir spent several days exploring the large fjord's various inlets and tributary glaciers. He was seeking evidence to prove his theory that Yosemite Valley in California was carved by the same powerful forces. Muir's writings caught the attention of scientists, one of whom was William Skinner Cooper, a botanist from the University of Minnesota. When Cooper arrived at Glacier Bay in 1916, he deemed it the best place on Earth to witness "plant succession," the study that explains how barren glacier-scrubbed rock can yield a lush, abundant evergreen forest over the course of just one century.

A century later, Glacier Bay's waters teem with humpback whales, orcas, sea otters, and sea lions; the spruce and hemlock forests are the habitat of brown bears, moose, and porcupine; and mountain goats inhabit the steep rocky cliffs in the upper bay. Overhead, bald eagles soar across the sky. Because of the park's variety of habitats and

SIZE OF PARK: 5,037 square miles (13,045 sq km) ★ **BEST TIME TO GO:** May to September
YEAR ESTABLISHED: 1980 ★ **IN-PARK ACCOMMODATIONS:** Lodges & camping

Kayak past floating icebergs within Glacier Bay.

lack of predators, more than 281 species of birds have been recorded in the park.

The abundance of wildlife is a prime draw for kayakers and cruise ship passengers. The other draw, of course, is the massive scenery, with the intimidating and remote 15,000-foot (4,572 m) peaks of the Fairweather Range looming in the distance to the west, and the more immediate

Steller sea lions lounge on South Marble Island, found along the Inside Passage of Glacier Bay.

Boardwalks lead through the coastal rainforest at Bartlett Cove.

The Tlingit totem pole honors the park's heritage.

thrill of the park's seven tidewater glaciers that calve dramatically into the bay, taking on a life of their own as chunks up to 200 feet (61 m) high crack and explode into the saltwater.

Start your visit at the Bartlett Cove visitors center, where the 20 foot tall (6.1 m), hand carved Huna Tlingit Healing Totem Pole commemorates the Tlingit's centuries of history in the region, which predates the Little Ice Age. The rules and regulations surrounding the establish-ment of the park strained the Tlingit way of life, and the pole is a symbolic gesture of healing between the two groups. ∎

66 The abundance of wildlife
is a prime draw
for kayakers and cruise ship
passengers. 99

KATMAI NATIONAL PARK AND PRESERVE

★★★★★★★★★★★★★★★★★★★★★★★★

In 1912, the largest volcanic eruption of the 20th century occurred in what is now Katmai National Park. A new volcano, later named Novarupta, spewed more than six cubic miles (25 cu km) of ash into the atmosphere, some of which fell back to earth as far away as Seattle. The explosion was so loud that residents of Juneau, 300 miles (482.8 km) to the southeast, heard it. After three days of eruptive activity, the Ukak River Valley was transformed into 40 square miles (103.6 sq km) of barren ash.

Luckily, the resident Alutiiq people, who made their home in the region, escaped the eruption without injury. But this giant blast, which was preceded by many small earthquakes in the days before the eruption, signaled to both people and animals that it was time to clear out.

On an expedition from the coast through the mountains in 1916, the scientist Robert F. Griggs discovered a portion of the Ukak River Valley that was so filled with superheated steam still escaping from thousands of fumaroles that he renamed it the Valley of Ten Thousand Smokes and lobbied President Woodrow Wilson to protect the region as a national park. The steam dissipated long ago, but the valley floor remains covered in a layer of ash and pumice hundreds of feet deep. The valley's landscape is so otherworldly that Apollo astronauts trained here prior to their lunar landing.

In addition to having more active volcanoes than any other U.S. national park, Katmai also has

SIZE OF PARK: 6,395 square miles (16,564 sq km) ★ **BEST TIME TO GO:** June to October
YEAR ESTABLISHED: 1918 ★ **IN-PARK ACCOMMODATIONS:** Lodges & camping

Emerald mountains
and aquamarine waters
are on offer in Katmai.

some of the highest densities of brown bears in the world. The best place to see them is in mid-July at Brooks Camp. The camp—an important archaeological site that has evidence of human history dating back 5,000 years—sits at the mouth of the Brooks River and along the shoreline of Naknek Lake. It has a number of viewing platforms from which to safely view bears, including one

Katmai was established in 1918 to protect the volcanically devastated region surrounding Novarupta and the Valley of Ten Thousand Smokes.

A one-of-a-kind-experience: Watching a brown bear fish for sockeye salmon at Brooks Falls within the national park

overlooking Brooks Falls, the famous drop-off where the ursine beasts vie for the best perch from which to catch airborne salmon as they try to swim upstream. With a lodge and a camp-ground, the site is an ideal base to access park hiking trails, including the 1.5-mile (2.4 km) hike to the overlook 800 feet (243.8 m) up Dumpling Mountain, which affords vast views of the park, and the more ambitious 23-mile (37 km) hike along a road through dense boreal forest that leads to the mystical Valley of Ten Thousand Smokes. ∎

> 66 Katmai also has some of the highest densities of brown bears in the world. 99

KENAI FJORDS NATIONAL PARK

★★★★★★★★★★★★★★★★★★★★★★★★

The beauty of Alaskan wilderness is that it's so vast that visitors can feel swallowed up by it. That can be overwhelming, especially for a first-time foray into the Last Frontier. Kenai Fjords National Park is the antidote. By no means small or tame, the park is only a 2.5-hour drive south of Anchorage on the Seward Highway, making it a great starter park for those who want to experience Alaska's largesse without the time, budget, or desire to go in too deep.

Fifty one percent of Kenai Fjords is covered in ice. Most of it is the 700-square-mile (1,813 sq km) Harding Icefield, which feeds the park's 38 glaciers. These massive slow-flowing ice rivers have retreated to form steep fjords and valleys, their bare rock colonized by mosses and lichens and brilliant purple fireweed. Because of its location on the edge of the North Pacific Ocean, the park is a haven for coastal Alaskan birds like peregrine falcons and horned puffins, as well as marine life like humpback whales, Steller sea lions, and Pacific white-sided dolphins.

Of the 38 glaciers, Exit Glacier, which has retreated 1.4 miles (2.3 km) since 1815, is the only one accessible by road. Ambitious hikers can tackle an 8.2-mile (13.2 km) round-trip journey on the Harding Icefield Trail, a rigorous climb that starts at the valley floor and winds through cottonwood and alder forests and meadows to above the tree line with a view of snow and ice. ∎

SIZE OF PARK: 1,047 square miles (2,711 sq km) ★ **BEST TIME TO GO:** June to August
YEAR ESTABLISHED: 1980 ★ **IN-PARK ACCOMMODATIONS:** Cabins & camping

Take in the icebergs on Bear Lake while stand-up paddleboarding through the crystal-blue waters.

KOBUK VALLEY NATIONAL PARK

★★★★★★★★★★★★★★★★★★★★★★★★★

"Now we were alone between fringes of spruce by a clear stream where tundra went up the sides of mountains," wrote John McPhee in *Coming into the Country*. The Kobuk Valley, he wrote, "was, in all likelihood, the most isolated wilderness I would ever see." Though this isolated national park north of the Arctic Circle in northwest Alaska is one of the least visited in the nation, the region has been inhabited by humans for more than 8,000 years.

Proof of the long history of human inhabitation is at Onion Portage, so named for the wild onions that grow at this long, narrow peninsula that juts out into the Kobuk River. For centuries, hundreds of thousands of caribou have used the peninsula located in the southeast corner of the park to cross the river on their biannual migration across the Brooks Range. Because swimming caribou are much slower than running caribou, hunters have followed the herd here. In the 1960s, archaeologists uncovered tools for hunting and fishing such as spear points and fishhooks from nine different cultures, evidence that the portage was used first as a seasonal campsite and later as a permanent home. These people were the earliest ancestors to the modern Inupiat, who still live in the valley, using practices handed down by their ancestors, such as cutting and drying salmon following the same methods that have been used for centuries.

SIZE OF PARK: 2,736 square miles (7,086 sq km) ★ BEST TIME TO GO: June to September
YEAR ESTABLISHED: 1980 ★ IN-PARK ACCOMMODATIONS: Camping

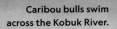
Caribou bulls swim across the Kobuk River.

HISTORICAL FOOTNOTE

In 1898, as the Klondike gold rush was beginning to wane, a prospector wrote a letter to the *San Francisco Chronicle* reporting that he found $50,000 (approximately $1.6 million today) in gold on the Kobuk River. The news created a stampede of 2,000 prospectors to the river, most of whom left empty-handed, but not before they whiled away time ice skating on the frozen water using repurposed saw blades for skates.

Among the most unique and surprising features in the park are the naturally occurring sand dunes. The sand—formed by the grinding of ancient glaciers during the last ice age and deposited in the valley by wind and water—are a sight straight out of Namibia. The largest of the three dune fields, Great Kobuk Sand Dunes, has 25 square miles (64.8 sq km) of golden sand that constantly shift a few miles south of the Kobuk River, rising 100 feet

A porcupine dries off next to the Kobuk River.

Autumn foliage decorates the park's Arctic tundra in a burst of color.

The 380-mile-long (611.6 km) Kobuk River offers dramatic views as well as fishing and floating opportunities.

(30.5 m) tall in some places. During the hottest summer months, the temperature in the park might reach an un-Alaskan 100°F (37.8°C).

When visiting Kobuk Valley National Park, it's important to add a few buffer days to the beginning and end of your trip. The park is accessible only by small planes, which can be vulnerable to unpredictable weather and other safety delays. ∎

> 66 Among the most unique and surprising features in the park are the naturally occurring sand dunes. 99

NATIONAL PARK OF AMERICAN SAMOA

★★★★★★★★★★★★★★★★★★★★★★★★★

Translated to English, Samoa means "sacred earth." It makes sense, then, that the only U.S. national park south of the Equator protects the lush tropical rainforests, stunning coral sand beaches, and surrounding waters of four remote volcanic South Pacific Islands: Tutuila, Ta'u, Ofu, and Olosega. The park also protects the archaeological and cultural resources of Polynesia's oldest culture. The first inhabitants of these islands arrived here from Asia 3,000 years ago.

With an average of 25,000 annual visitors, the park is a paradise for divers, snorkelers, and beach lovers in search of the quintessential castaway experience. Visitors to the park won't be served umbrella drinks by the pool. There is little in the way of tourism infrastructure here. No camping is allowed, and the only lodging within park boundaries is through a homestay—a cultural exchange in which guests stay in a Samoan house, or *fale*, eat with their Samoan hosts, and participate in village activities such as cutting pandanus leaves to dry for weaving mats.

It's a rich experience, but one that requires a few ground rules. To have a harmonious stay, it's important that visitors respect the Samoan way, or *fa'asamoa*. A few tenants of *fa'asamoa* are: When staying in a *fale*, one must sit down on the floor with legs covered before talking, eating, or drinking. In the evenings, villagers observe a prayer time known as *sa*. If a guest happens to

---

SIZE OF PARK: 21.09 square miles (54.6 sq km) ★ **BEST TIME TO GO:** Year-round
YEAR ESTABLISHED: 1988 ★ **IN-PARK ACCOMMODATIONS:** Homestay lodging

Snorkel along a pristine coral reef just off the shore of Ofu Island.

In 2020, the U.S. Treasury came out with a new collection of coins paying tribute to the National Park System. One features a Samoan fruit bat mother hanging in a tree with her pups. The coin is meant to draw attention to this gravely endangered species. It is not, as some believe, a clue to the conspiracy theory that posits the U.S. government was aware of COVID-19 before it warned its citizens.

be entering the village during *sa*, it's important to stop and allow the worshippers to complete the prayers before entering. And Sunday is for church and rest, not for swimming.

On any other day, however, the park's vivid underwater terrain is open for exploration. With 2,550 acres (1,032 ha) of coral reefs, it is a magical playground teeming with 950 species of fish. The best snorkeling is off the island of Ofu, which

Kingfishers are just one of hundreds of birds seen throughout the park.

A man prepares for a traditional *umu* celebratory feast.

South Pacific waters and vibrant green jungle landscapes are ripe for exploring throughout the National Park of American Samoa.

> 66 Time a visit in September or October and humpback whales, who give birth to their young here, might be breaching offshore. 99

requires hiring a local fisherman from the island of Ta'u who may be willing to take you there by boat. The logistics are worth it. Time a visit in September or October and humpback whales, who give birth to their young here, might be breaching offshore.

Keep in mind the importance of protecting this park while you're enjoying it. With every passing year the reef, which contains 250 species of coral, is feeling the effects of climate change. Warmer temperatures in water near shore has increased coral bleaching and disease. ∎

WAR IN THE PACIFIC NATIONAL HISTORIC PARK

★★★★★★★★★★★★★★★★★★★★★★★★

Guam is a lush, 212-square-mile (549.1 sq km) peanut-shaped tropical oasis that is the largest and southernmost island in the Mariana chain. When snorkeling its coral reefs that flit with brilliantly colored fish or exploring its interior of tropical savanna grasslands, limestone forests, and coastal wetlands, it's hard to imagine how such an idyll could play such an outsize role in World War II.

Shortly after their attack on Pearl Harbor, the Japanese invaded Guam. Marine captain George J. McMillan, fearful that a prolonged fight with no immediate reinforcement would cause worse suffering for the 10,000 Guamanians and U.S. forces stationed there, surrendered. The Japanese subjected the residents, most of whom were descendants of the Indigenous Chamorro people, into forced labor, torture, and execution. On July 21, 1944, the United States launched a successful 21-day campaign to liberate Guam. The resulting death toll for the Japanese was 18,000, exponentially higher than the 1,700 others who lost their lives. The park commemorates the bravery and sacrifice of all the soldiers who participated in the vast Pacific Theater of World War II. ■

SIZE OF PARK: 3 square miles (7.76 sq km) ★ **BEST TIME TO GO:** Year-round
YEAR ESTABLISHED: 1978 ★ **IN-PARK ACCOMMODATIONS:** None

The honor guard stands in formation, flags flying, on Memorial Day.

HAWAII VOLCANOES NATIONAL PARK

★★★★★★★★★★★★★★★★★★★★★★★★★

Sacred home to Madame Pele, the goddess of volcanoes and fire who created the Hawaiian Islands, this national park in the middle of the Pacific Ocean is one of the few places on the planet where it's possible to see the primordial forces of Earth simultaneously create and destroy. Pele is known to Hawaiians, after all, as "she who shapes the sacred land."

On the island of Hawaii, the park rises from sea level to 13,677 feet (4,168.8 m) and contains the summits of two of the most active volcanoes on Earth—Mauna Loa and Kilauea. The 1868 eruption of Mauna Loa triggered hundreds of earthquakes, a tsunami, and a landslide that ultimately killed 77 Hawaiians. The 1983 eruption of Pu'u 'Ō'ō on the eastern shoulder of Kilauea was less forceful, but it lasted 35 years. Pele's dwelling place, Halema'uma'u crater, at the summit of Kilauea, has a long history of eruptions. A lake inside the summit crater that measured 160 feet (48.8 m) deep and held 165 million gallons of water was instantly vaporized by molten lava after a December 20, 2020, summit eruption.

The land that Pele's powerful forces created contains almost every climate on Earth, from ocean to alpine to rainforest to desert. Hawaiians have more than 200 words for "rain" alone depending on its color, duration, intensity, the angles along which it falls, and the seasons in which it falls. Their intense relationship with

---

SIZE OF PARK: 505 square miles (1,307.9 sq km) ★ **BEST TIME TO GO:** Year-round
YEAR ESTABLISHED: 1916 ★ **IN-PARK ACCOMMODATIONS:** Lodges & camping

Lava from Kilauea spills into the ocean, continuing to expand the park's landscape.

The Puna Coast Trail leads to the beach at Halape, which is also a federally protected turtle nesting sanctuary.

WILDLIFE SIGHTING

The ancestors of the 'ōpe'ape'a, or the Hawaiian hoary bat, the only remaining native land mammal in Hawaii, arrived on the island 10,000 years ago, and the species is now listed as endangered. Of the 1,300 bat species on the planet, its journey across 2,000 miles (3,218.7 km) of ocean is the longest overwater flight that resulted in the populating of a new species.

nature is deeply tied to their practice of Malama 'Aina, or "care for the land." This practice goes far beyond preservation and stewardship. It is a reverence for the surroundings they are so privileged to inhabit, which is why it is essential that visitors to Hawaii Volcanoes National Park respect not only the park but also give space and privacy to Hawaiians who are there to offer gifts to Pele.

Ninety percent of the park's plant and animal species are endemic, which makes it a fascinating evolutionary frontier. The nēnē—the official state bird of Hawaii—is the world's rarest goose that has a shared ancestor with the Canada goose, albeit with less webbed feet, shorter necks, and a plumage more suitable for hot climates. At the time of Captain Cook's arrival in 1778, there were approximately 25,000 nēnē. By the 1940s, that number had dwindled to 50. The birds have since rebounded but are a constant symbol of the tenuous existence of many of Hawaii's native birds.

The park has more than 150 miles (241.4 km) of wildly diverse backcountry trails: The popular 'Āpua Point trail hugs the coastline and traverses over ropy pahoehoe, or basaltic lava, flows and sand dunes for 6.6 miles (10.6 km) to a grove of coconut trees where hikers can camp overnight. The other extreme is a hike to the 13,678-foot (4,169.1 m) summit of Mauna Loa, a trail carved out of jagged lava by Buffalo Soldiers who were assigned to assist park founder and geologist Thomas Jaggar in building the world's first volcano observatory in 1915.

Hiking to the top of the world's largest active volcano is no easy feat. It requires at least a few days to properly acclimate to and navigate the extremely rugged terrain, which includes high altitude, frequent fog, wind and cold, and sometimes loose lava rocks. At the top is a summit cabin, potentially snow, and, if you're lucky, a spectacular sunrise view. ■

BY THE NUMBERS: 2018 KILAUEA ERUPTION

2: Number of places it erupted
13.7: Square miles (35.5 sq km) the lava flow covered
700: Number of homes destroyed
875: Acres (354.1 ha) the lava added to the island of Hawaii
2,000: Number of people the eruption displaced
60,000: Number of earthquakes triggered

Hike along cooled pahoehoe lava flows throughout the park.

A showcase of the park's diverse foliage, tropical rainforest sprawls near the Thurston Lava Tube.

HALEAKALĀ NATIONAL PARK

★★★★★★★★★★★★★★★★★★★★★★★★★

Haleakalā, or "House of the Sun," has been a spiritual centerpiece for Native Hawaiians for at least a thousand years. Never a place of permanent habitation, the rim of the dormant shield volcano, which lies 10,023 feet (3,055 m) above sea level, is part of *wao akua,* or the realm of the gods, a sacred place to honor the deities and bid farewell to the deceased. The volcano's last eruption is estimated to have occurred 400 to 600 years ago, between 1480 and 1600.

The resulting crater is a dynamic landscape with red cinder cones and black lava beds inhabited by Haleakalā silversword, a yucca-like plant that can take a half century to flower; and nēnē, the endangered black-headed Hawaiian goose. There are 30 miles (48.3 km) of hiking trails to explore within the crater, but be prepared for ever changing weather that ranges from bright sunshine and 80°F (26.7°C) to rain and sleet and 30°F (-1.1°C). Many people time their visit with a spectacular sunrise over the crater rim, which requires online reservations a week in advance. The 3 a.m. wakeup call is worth it.

The tropical side of the park can be found close to the end of the 52-mile-long (83.7 km) Hana Highway, a curvaceous nail-biter with 59 bridges that hugs Maui's pristine northeastern shoreline. Just past the town of Hāna is the park's Kīpahulu District, a paradise of 400-foot-high (121.9 m) waterfalls, bamboo forests, and brilliant flowers like the flaming red ones found on the 'ōhi'a tree. ■

SIZE OF PARK: 52 square miles (134 sq km) ★ **BEST TIME TO GO:** Year-round
YEAR ESTABLISHED: 1961 ★ **IN-PARK ACCOMMODATIONS:** Camping & three rustic cabins

After sunrise, hike down Haleakalā to take in the otherworldly volcanic landscape.

NĀPALI COAST STATE WILDERNESS PARK

★★★★★★★★★★★★★★★★★★★★★★★★

With fluted emerald peaks, omnipresent crashing surf, and 100-foot-high (30.5 m) cascading waterfalls, Kauai's rugged and roadless Nāpali Coast feels like a landscape from a lost world. It's hard to believe that, until a century ago, this seemingly uninhabitable coastline was occupied for at least 1,000 years by Hawaiians who farmed taro, coffee, and oranges; fished in the Pacific; and built temples and shrines to their deities.

The 11-mile-long (17.7 km) Kalalau Trail, which traverses the precipitous mountainside and crosses five valleys before ending at Kalalau Beach, was built in the 1860s in order to foster a means of transportation for their cattle and horses, helping to facilitate commerce for the isolated people living here. Remains of the former inhabitants exist today in the form of irrigation ditches, terraced fields, house platforms, temples, shrines, and graves. Many of these ancient sites were designed in such harmony with the landscape and have since been covered in lush vegetation that they are almost invisible to the untrained eye.

In recent years, the trail through this tropical paradise has attracted three-quarters of a million annual visitors who take on the most challenging hike in the Hawaiian Islands to reap its robust rewards, which include beaches like Hanakapiai, waterfalls like 500-foot (152.4 m) Hanakoa, and a campsite on the yellow-sand Kalalau Beach.

SIZE OF PARK: 9.6 square miles (25 sq km) ★ **BEST TIME TO GO:** May to October
YEAR ESTABLISHED: 1983 ★ **IN-PARK ACCOMMODATIONS:** Camping

The Kalalau hiking trail offers scenic over-looks to views of Nāpali's colorful coastline.

THE CHALLENGE

Because the park has suffered from illegal camping, damage to historical ruins, and other ills of over-tourism, it is imperative that visitors practice impeccable leave-no-trace wilderness ethics when visiting. That includes packing out what you pack in, camping legally, and not disturbing what centuries have created.

In April 2018, a series of thunderstorms produced record-breaking rainfall on Kauai's north shore. Almost 50 inches (127 cm) of rain fell in 24 hours, marking the most severe rain event in the islands since records started being kept in 1905. As a result, the park was closed for almost a year and the only road accessing it—the Kuhio Highway—was badly damaged. Park officials used the

Wailua Falls cascades in two streams, plummeting 173 feet (52.7 m), and was featured in the opening credits of *Fantasy Island*.

Nāpali Coast State Wilderness Park offers stunning ocean views.

Trail markers guide your way along Kalalau from Ke'e Beach.

closure to implement new policies around visiting the Nāpali Coast State Wilderness Park in order to try to mitigate cultural and environmental damage from overtourism.

To visit the trail today requires advanced planning. Day hikers are allowed to travel as far as two miles (3.2 km) in to Hanakapiai Beach without a permit but still need to make reservations in advance to enter Hā'ena State Park, where the trailhead for Kalalau Trail is located. Overnight campers are required to apply for a permit months in advance. The planning is worth the effort. Currently only 60 people are allowed on the trail at one time, which allows every hiker to experience the expansive beauty of the Nāpali Coast in relative solitude. ∎

66 Kauai's rugged and roadless Nāpali Coast feels like a landscape from a lost world. 99

PEARL HARBOR NATIONAL MEMORIAL

★★★★★★★★★★★★★★★★★★★★★★★★

Pearl Harbor is a stunning port of turquoise water lined by verdant mountains on the island of Oahu. On December 7, 1941, 2,335 U.S. military servicemen and women and 68 civilians were killed, and another 1,178 were wounded during the imperial Japanese attack on this idyllic harbor. The beginning of U.S. involvement in World War II, the deadliest conflict in human history that ultimately resulted in the deaths of 70 to 85 million people, lasted one hour and 15 minutes.

The iconic white concrete memorial that spans the sunken U.S.S. *Arizona* is a widely recognized symbol of Pearl Harbor. Austrian-born American architect Alfred Preis, who was detained for three months at a Honolulu incarceration camp for Japanese Americans and German Americans after the attack, designed the memorial. The 29,630-ton battleship it commemorates was struck at 8:10 a.m. by a 1,760-pound (800 kg) bomb. The massive explosion caused the ship's munitions and fuels to ignite, creating such additional force that the ship reportedly rose out of the water before sinking to a depth of 40 feet (12.2 m) and killing 1,177 crew members on board. The ship's hull is still a tomb for more than 900 of those sailors and also serves a new purpose as an artificial reef that provides a habitat for marine life.

In addition to the U.S.S. *Arizona*, the memorial includes the lesser known but equally important sunken wrecks of the U.S.S. *Utah*, the first ship

---

SIZE OF PARK: 10.5 acres (4.2 ha) ★ **BEST TIME TO GO:** Year-round
YEAR ESTABLISHED: 1962 ★ **IN-PARK ACCOMMODATIONS:** None

A naval special warfare sailor floats a traditional lei near the U.S.S. *Arizona* Memorial during a Remembrance Day ceremony.

struck by Japanese planes on which 58 crew members died, and the U.S.S. *Oklahoma,* a battleship that was struck by nine Japanese torpedoes during the first 10 minutes of the attack, killing 429 sailors. Six additional concrete mooring quays commemorate the location of other battleships stationed on Battleship Row in the harbor during the time of the attack.

Memorial plaques honor lives lost in the attack on Pearl Harbor.

Look at the wreckage from the U.S.S. *Arizona* Memorial.

Huge cannons front the U.S.S. *Missouri*, docked in Pearl Harbor.

66 The ship's hull is still a tomb for more than 900 of those sailors
and also serves a new purpose
as an artificial reef that provides a habitat for marine life. 99

On Ford Island, a still active military installation in Pearl Harbor, there are six historical petty officer bungalows that are part of the memorial. These former residences were so close to the U.S.S. *Ari-zona* when it exploded that silverware expelled from the ship was reportedly lodged into their exteriors. From these bungalows able-bodied military triaged the casualties from *Arizona*'s hull. ■

VIRGIN ISLANDS NATIONAL PARK

★★★★★★★★★★★★★★★★★★★★★★★★★

In September 2017, twin hurricanes Irma and Maria devastated the Caribbean island of St. John. The formerly idyllic oasis, 73 percent of which is Virgin Islands National Park, renowned worldwide for its shimmering white-sand beaches, precipitous forested peaks, and turquoise waters, was transformed overnight.

Irma's 185-mile-an-hour (297.7 km/h) winds blew leaves off most trees, toppled telephone poles, sunk or washed ashore 90 vessels, destroyed park infrastructure, and badly damaged coral reefs offshore. Two weeks later, Maria rolled through, her 155-mile-an-hour (249.5 km/h) winds further pummeling the island, causing heavy rainfall that created landslides and left residents without power.

The dual hurricanes created unimaginable loss for the 5,000 residents of St. John and the National Park Service, especially underwater, where the coral reefs—some of which are 600 years old and grow less than one centimeter per year—may never fully recover. On land, however, recovery efforts were heroic. The U.S. Navy, National Guard, and Department of Interior teams, along with groups like Friends of Virgin Islands National Park, worked for months to clear debris, rebuild trails, and repair buildings.

Virgin Islands National Park sprawls across most of the island. Hiking trails traverse steep terrain through one of the last remaining dry tropical rainforests in the Caribbean. Visitors can sun,

---

SIZE OF PARK: 23 square miles (60 sq km) ★ **BEST TIME TO GO:** Year-round
YEAR ESTABLISHED: 1956 ★ **IN-PARK ACCOMMODATIONS:** Camping

Palm trees line the sandy beaches of Maho Bay in St. John.

swim, stand-up paddleboard (SUP), and snorkel among sea turtles and colorful marine fish—there are 400 species in the park—off iconic white-sand beaches like Maho Bay and Trunk Bay.

Amid the park's beauty are remnants of a complex human history that began 3,000 years ago when the first people arrived on the island from South America. Between 500 and 1,000 years ago, the Taíno, who had their own language and worshipped gods known as zemis,

Sailboats anchor in Cruz Bay, off the coast of St. John in Virgin Islands National Park.

Visit the ruins of the Annaberg Sugar Plantation boiling room, a relic of the island's complicated past, found within the park boundaries.

settled on St. John. In 1718, the Danish claimed the island, and by 1728, European settlers had built 100 sugar plantations. For seven months in 1733, enslaved plantation workers took over the island with the intent of creating the first free African state in the Americas. French forces from neighboring Martinique quelled the rebellion. By the time the fighting was over, 300 enslaved people and more than three-quarters of the European settlers had been killed. More than 100 years later, in 1848, the enslaved people of the Danish West Indies were emancipated. ■

66 Amid the park's beauty are remnants of a complex human history that began 3,000 years ago. 99

SAN JUAN NATIONAL HISTORIC SITE

★★★★★★★★★★★★★★★★★★★★★★★★★

Puerto Rico played a critical strategic role for Spain from the time Christopher Columbus set foot on the island in 1493 until they ceded it to the United States under the provisions of the 1898 Treaty of Paris, which ended the Spanish-American War. The easternmost of the Greater Antilles, the island was the first major oasis after a long Atlantic crossing where ships could resupply.

As the Spanish expanded their empire into Mexico and Central and South America, Puerto Rico became the ideal entry point to the New World, a place from which to defend the riches of their new colonies. To do so, they fortified San Juan with seemingly impenetrable walls and structures. The remains of this fortified system are now San Juan National Historic Site, which includes Castillo San Felipe del Morro ("El Morro") and Castillo San Cristóbal; a portion of the walls surrounding the old city; and Fort San Juan de la Cruz.

The most iconic of these sites is El Morro, the fortress that sits on a 140-foot (42.7 m) promontory at the entrance to San Juan Bay. Construction began in 1539 and was completed 251 years later, in 1790. With six levels overlooking the Atlantic, soldiers could fire a powerful barrage of artillery at oncoming ships. The fortress was so intimidating that it had a reputation as being unconquerable. Four centuries later, it's still a haunting visual reinforcement of the power of the Spanish colonizers. ■

SIZE OF PARK: 75 acres (30.3 ha) ★ **BEST TIME TO GO:** April to June
YEAR ESTABLISHED: 1949 ★ **IN-PARK ACCOMMODATIONS:** None

El Morro, built to protect Old San Juan, is a must-visit for insight into Puerto Rico's history.

PART THREE

THE EAST & MID-ATLANTIC

Grass-covered sand dunes line Marconi Beach on Cape Cod National Seashore (p. 232).

WEIR FARM NATIONAL HISTORICAL PARK

★★★★★★★★★★★★★★★★★★★★★★★

Unlike many aspiring artists, Julian Alden Weir had the blessing of his father, Robert Walter Weir, a professor of drawing at the U.S. Military Academy, to pursue his passion. In 1873, when the 17-year-old Weir went off to study at the École des Beaux-Arts in Paris, his father told him, "Don't return, old boy, until your veins flow with the rich mother's milk of Art, fatten on it, and then let your own genius ripen with the experience of it."

Weir took those words to heart, eventually becoming a beloved American Impressionist. His evolution as an artist is largely thanks to his Connecticut farm, which he bought for the sum of $10, and a painting he had acquired in Europe from the art dealer Erwin Davis in 1882. Weir painted, hunted, fished, and philosophized here with a revolving door of famous artists, including Albert Pinkham Ryder, John Henry Twachtman, Childe Hassam, and John Singer Sargent.

When he died of heart disease in 1919, Weir's daughter Dorothy Weir Young, also a painter, lived on the farm with her husband, the sculptor Mahonri Young. After Young's death, New England artists Doris and Sperry Andrews bought the farm and painted here until 2005. Visitors to the farm can view the sites where more than 250 works of art were created, tour Weir's home and the artists' studios, or carry on the rich legacy by painting their own masterpiece. ■

SIZE OF PARK: 68 acres (27 ha) ★ **BEST TIME TO GO:** May to October
YEAR ESTABLISHED: 1990 ★ **IN-PARK ACCOMMODATIONS:** None

Weir Farm was the home
of Impressionist
painter J. Alden Weir
until his death in 1919.

BOMBAY HOOK NATIONAL WILDLIFE REFUGE

★★★★★★★★★★★★★★★★★★★★★★★★

In 1679, Mechacksett, the chief of the Kahansink, sold this saltwater marsh, known as Canaresse or "shaggy bushes," to Peter Bayard of New York. The alleged sale price was one gun, four handfuls of powder, three waistcoats, liquor, and a kettle. The ensuing Dutch settlers, who called it Bompies Hoeck, or "little-tree point," used it to cut salt hay, trap muskrats, and hunt waterfowl.

Two and a half centuries later, in 1938, an all-Black company from the Civilian Conservation Corps labored for four years to prepare the marshland as a refuge for migratory waterfowl, one chain in a link of refuges that now stretch from Canada to the Gulf of Mexico.

Today, Bombay Hook is one of more than 567 national wildlife refuges managed by the U.S. Fish and Wildlife Service and the largest remaining expanse of tidal salt marsh in the mid-Atlantic. Every year hundreds of thousands of birds migrate through, from shorebirds in May that stop to feed on horseshoe crab eggs; to herons, egrets, and glossy ibis during the summer months; to more than 150,000 ducks and geese flying south in November and December. In total, more than 300 species of birds have been recorded here.

Visitors can drive a round-trip loop around Raymond, Shearness, and Bear Swamp Pools; hike one of five short trails in the refuge; or climb one of three observation towers to better see and photograph the spectacular winged array. ∎

SIZE OF PARK: 25 square miles (64.66 sq km) ★ BEST TIME TO GO: Year-round
YEAR ESTABLISHED: 1937 ★ IN-PARK ACCOMMODATIONS: None

A young great egret perches on a thin branch in the Bombay Hook preserve.

ACADIA NATIONAL PARK

★★★★★★★★★★★★★★★★★★★★★★★★★

"The mountain summits are all bare and rocky ... I name it Isles des Monts Déserts," wrote French explorer Samuel de Champlain in 1604. Today, most Mainers pronounce the crown jewel of Acadia National Park "Mount *Dessert*," but its original name is Pemetic, or Range of Mountains, the name given by its original Wabanaki inhabitants, who have been here for 12,000 years.

The four tribes comprising Maine's Wabanaki, or "the people of the dawn"—the Maliseet, Micmac, Penobscot, and Passamaquoddy—have used the island for millennia to trade, hunt, fish, and dig for clams at Moneskatik, or "the clam digging place," which is now the town of Bar Harbor. Some Wabanaki still gather ash splint and sweetgrass on the island and weave it into beautifully complex baskets, many of which can be seen at Bar Harbor's Abbe Museum, a partner to the Smithsonian Institution.

More recent human history of Acadia National Park—the first to be designated east of the Mississippi River—is evident throughout its rocky coastal landscape. The park spreads across portions of Isle au Haut, Mount Desert Island, and the Schoodic Peninsula to the north. In the early 1800s, Irishman John Carroll carved out a homestead on the west side of Mount Desert Island near the present-day town of Somesville. His family's back-breaking labor is still evident at the Carroll Homestead, where three generations of Carrolls lived

SIZE OF PARK: 65 square miles (168 sq km) ★ **BEST TIME TO GO:** Year-round
YEAR ESTABLISHED: 1919 ★ **IN-PARK ACCOMMODATIONS:** Camping

Acadia's Bass Harbor Head
Light Station was added
to the National Register of
Historic Places in 1988.

into the 1900s. Their simple shingle-sided residence with no running water, electricity, or gas lighting still stands, giving Acadia's annual four million visitors the opportunity to glimpse the hard life of a homesteader 200 years ago.

In the early 1900s, the philanthropist John D. Rockefeller, Jr., an accomplished horseman, wanted a way to explore the island without a car. Between 1913 and 1940, he funded 45 miles (72.4 km) of carriage roads. These 16-foot-wide (4.9 m) stone pathways were works of beauty, featuring ornate, arched stone bridges spanning rivers and overlooking waterfalls, as well as granite coping, stones known as Rockefeller's teeth, lining each road. Cyclists, hikers, horseback riders, and cross-country skiers still use the roads, traveling through spruce-filled forests, stands of New England hardwoods, and 1,600-foot-tall (487.7 m)

Autumn colors burst to life in Carrying Place Inlet, just outside Acadia National Park in Hancock, Maine.

Take in sweeping views from the summit of Cadillac Mountain on Mount Desert Island.

granite peaks to views of the sunrise over the North Atlantic.

For burgeoning car enthusiasts, Rockefeller also funded a 27-mile-long (43.5 km) road on both the Schoodic Peninsula and Mount Desert Island. Construction on the island's Park Loop Road began in 1927. Its final segment was completed 31 years later, in 1958. ∎

HISTORICAL FOOTNOTE

Before there were Instagram influencers, there were "rusticators." These painters from the mid-1800s, like Thomas Cole and Frederic Church from the Hudson River School, created beautiful renditions of Mount Desert Island that inspired visitors to flock there in steamboats and yachts, which ignited tourism and, ultimately, the establishment of the park.

HARRIET TUBMAN UNDERGROUND RAILROAD NATIONAL HISTORICAL PARK

★★★★★★★★★★★★★★★★★★★★★★★★★

It's no accident that the modern interpretive buildings at this newly established national park on Maryland's Eastern Shore are oriented north. Harriet Tubman spent the majority of her life fighting for justice and freedom that could only be found at a higher latitude.

In 1849, only five feet tall (1.5 m), 27 years old, and alone, Tubman used the skills she had learned while working in the marshes of Maryland to navigate her way to freedom in Philadelphia. Tubman never wanted to be separated from her family again, so she returned to Maryland 13 times between 1850 and 1860 to lead 70 enslaved peoples, including her brothers, parents, and other friends and family members to freedom. Tubman used ingenious techniques to avoid her capture, which would have brought a $4,000 reward. And in 1863, while working as a nurse, cook, Union Army scout, and spy, Tubman led a raid along the Combahee River that contributed to freeing another 750 enslaved.

Tubman ultimately settled in Auburn, New York, where she married a Civil War veteran, Nelson Davis; adopted a daughter, Gertie; established the Home for the Aged; and co-founded the National Association of Colored Women. Auburn's Harriet Tubman National Historical Park, a companion monument to the one in Maryland, highlights Tubman's Underground Railroad work and the years after she became free.

SIZE OF PARK: .75 square mile (1.9 sq km) ★ BEST TIME TO GO: Year-round
YEAR ESTABLISHED: 2017 ★ IN-PARK ACCOMMODATIONS: None

Stewart's Canal was dug by enslaved and free Blacks between 1810 and 1832.

The park in Maryland focuses on Tubman's life of slavery, from when she was born into it in 1822 until she emancipated herself 27 years later. In addition to seeing the powerful displays in the interpretive center, visitors can meander the legacy garden and make their way to surrounding historic sites like Stewart's Canal, a seven-mile-long (11.3 km) waterway built by enslaved people and free men, where Tubman and her father worked floating timber and other goods to ships at nearby wharves.

To continue the tour, guests can drive the 125-mile-long (201.2 km) Harriet Tubman Underground Railroad Byway to Philadelphia. One important site near the park is the Bucktown Village Store, a local market where Tubman almost lost her life as a young girl when she refused to help an overseer stop a freedom-seeking individual. To stop the runaway, the overseer threw a two-pound (0.9 kg) weight that hit Tubman's head. It cracked her skull, but Tubman was forced to return to work with blood caking around the wound. The resulting epileptic seizures lasted Tubman's entire life. ■

WILDLIFE SIGHTING

The 30,000-plus-acre (12,1440.6 ha) Blackwater National Wildlife Refuge is adjacent to the park and gives guests a sense of the land in which Tubman hid from her captors and traveled through to rescue her friends and family. Today the refuge contains one of the highest concentrations of nesting bald eagles on the Atlantic coast.

Tubman returned to Maryland's Eastern Shore at least 13 times, helping to free more than 70 people.

"I prayed to God to make me strong and able to fight, and that's what I've always prayed for ever since."

– Harriet Tubman, 1865

BOSTON NATIONAL HISTORICAL PARK

★★★★★★★★★★★★★★★★★★★★★★★

No place more vividly recounts the epic saga of the American Revolution than Boston's Freedom Trail. The well-marked 2.5-mile-long (4 km) path clearly lays out the country's transition from a British colony to an independent nation.

Linking together seven of the eight official sites that make up Boston National Historical Park, the trail zigzags from the visitors center in Boston Common, the oldest public park in the United States; passes the home of Paul Revere, the silversmith who made his fateful midnight ride on April 18, 1775; crosses the Charles River to the Charlestown Navy Yard, which, for 174 years, repaired, modernized, and resupplied ships; and ends at Bunker Hill Monument, a memorial to the lives lost on June 17, 1775, in the Battle of Bunker Hill.

One of the more thought-provoking sites along the trail is Faneuil Hall, the "Cradle of Liberty," and a central gathering place for Revolutionary-era meetings and protests. Its namesake, Peter Faneuil, the wealthy merchant who donated the hall, made his fortune off the slave trade.

Nearby, but not officially part of Boston National Historical Park, is the 1.6-mile (2.6 km) Black Heritage Trail in Boston's Beacon Hill neighborhood. It pays homage to the Black community that lived here and, even before the Civil War, organized for equal rights and education, championed the movement to abolish slavery, and housed those who sought freedom through the Underground Railroad. ■

SIZE OF PARK: 43 acres (17 ha) ★ **BEST TIME TO GO:** Year-round
YEAR ESTABLISHED: 1974 ★ **IN-PARK ACCOMMODATIONS:** None

Faneuil Hall hosted America's first town meeting, playing a pivotal role in the Revolution.

CAPE COD NATIONAL SEASHORE

★★★★★★★★★★★★★★★★★★★★★★★★★

The wind, water, and waves along this magical 40-mile (64.4 km) stretch of Atlantic seashore seem to have the intoxicating effect of scrubbing the spirit clean. "The sea-shore is a sort of neutral ground, a most advantageous point from which to contemplate this world," Henry David Thoreau wrote of Cape Cod in the 1850s.

Mary Oliver, the poet who lived most of her adult life in the Cape towns of Truro and Province-town, elevated the simplicity of the natural life she found here—from hermit crabs to mollusks to geese to sunsets—into literary genius.

The intrepid writer Paul Theroux, who paddled the treacherous waters around the entire Cape in his kayak, wrote in his book of essays *Fresh Air Fiend,* "the word 'landscape' presents a problem on the Cape. I find it hard to separate the land from the water, or the water from the winds." To have such a wild connection to nature so close to the crowded cities of Boston and New York was a gift not lost on President John F. Kennedy, himself a longtime summer resident of the Cape. In 1961, he authorized the establishment of Cape Cod National Seashore. At the time, the legislation was an innovative approach for creating a park between towns and privately owned land.

The ways to experience the seashore are many and some of the most beautiful sites are also linked to a crucial moment in American history. Hike the 1.3-mile-long (2.1 km) loop inland trail through oak forest in Truro to Pilgrim Spring,

SIZE OF PARK: 68 square miles (176 sq km) ★ BEST TIME TO GO: Summer or fall
YEAR ESTABLISHED: 1961 ★ IN-PARK ACCOMMODATIONS: None

Nauset Beach Light was erected in 1923, using the 1877 tower moved to Nauset Beach from Chatham.

WILDLIFE SIGHTING

In recent years, the seal population near the seashore has increased, which has in turn increased the population of native great white sharks. While it's rare for a great white to bite a human, five swimmers since 2012 have been bitten in the waters off Cape Cod, one of whom died in 2018.

where the *Mayflower* pilgrims found their first fresh water in the new world in November 1620. Or walk the seemingly endless miles of Marconi Beach, so named for Guglielmo Marconi, the Italian inventor who transmitted the first transatlantic radio messages from the president of the United States to the king of England at nearby Wellfleet

Marconi Beach harbors several rare species, including broom crowberry and two types of poverty grass.

Cape Cod National Seashore spans 40 miles (64.4 km), offering plentiful beach hiking opportunities.

station in 1903. The 40-foot (12.2 m) dunes behind the beach were the ideal open space from which to submit the signal. At the very northern tip of the Cape sits Old Harbor Life-Saving Station, relocated from the eroding shoreline in Chatham, where it was used by the United States Life-Saving Service, and then by its successor, the United States Coast Guard, at the turn of the 19th century as a place from which to deploy small rescue crews by surfboat to rescue shipwrecked sailors. ∎

66 The ways to experience the seashore are many. 99

WHITE MOUNTAIN NATIONAL FOREST

★★★★★★★★★★★★★★★★★★★★★★★★

White Mountain National Forest is a good place to ponder the modern-day meaning of "wilderness." Within its more than 1,000 square miles (2,590 sq km) of mountains, rivers, lakes, trees, and peaks that sprawl across eastern New Hampshire and western Maine, the forest has six designated wilderness areas.

According to the 1964 Wilderness Act, a "wilderness" is an area "where the earth and its community of life are untrammeled by man." But ironically, the largest wilderness in this northeast complex, 45,000-acre (18,210.9 ha) Pemigewassett, once contained 72 miles (115.9 km) of train lines. Between 1880 and 1940, logging companies removed more than one million board feet (304,800 m) of timber from the surrounding 66,000-acre (26,709.2 ha) watershed. A fire that raged on for 10 days in 1907 furthered the already significant damage. Thankfully, in the 120 years since, especially after being designated a wilderness area in 1984, Pemigewassett has been a model of resilience, sprouting a new hardwood forest protected by mountains with not a road in sight. But its history is a reminder that very little of the United States' 174,000-plus square miles (450,657.9 sq km) of designated wilderness has actually been untouched by humans. This forest has been inhabited for 10,000 years, as evidenced by the 21 prehistoric Native American sites and several 19th-century buildings—including the 1832 Russell-Colbath House, a classic example

SIZE OF PARK: 1,225 square miles (3,172 sq km) ★ **BEST TIME TO GO:** Year-round
YEAR ESTABLISHED: 1918 ★ **IN-PARK ACCOMMODATIONS:** Lodges & camping

Look out over the White Mountains and autumnal forests from Franconia Notch State Park.

of a century-old family farm—found within its borders.

Today, visitors use the forest for inspiration, recreation, and solitude: In the autumn, the hardwood foliage flames in brilliant yellows, oranges, and reds along the 34-mile-long (54.7 km) Kancamagus Scenic Byway from Conway to Lincoln. In the summer, hard-core hikers tackle

Winter landscapes in New Hampshire's White Mountains are just as beautiful as summer and fall scenery.

Take a guided train tour on Mount Washington's Cog Railway.

Mount Washington is famous for extreme weather at its summit.

> ❝ Its history is a reminder that very little of the United States' … designated wilderness has actually been untouched by humans. ❞

the 89.5-mile (144 km) portion of the Appalachian Trail, which climbs a brutal 32,191 feet (9,811.8 m) from Glencliff in the southwest to Gorham in the northeast. In the winter, eight Nordic and alpine ski resorts host more than a million visitors.

The king of the forest is 6,288-foot (1,916.6 m) Mount Washington. The highest peak in the northeastern United States, Washington is one of the deadliest in the world, largely because it sits at the nexus where jet stream storms, which move west to east and southwest to northeast, meet weather systems that move up and down the Atlantic Coast. The highest wind velocity ever recorded, 231 miles an hour (371.8 km/h), was logged at its summit on April 12, 1934. ■

DELAWARE WATER GAP NATIONAL RECREATION AREA

★★★★★★★★★★★★★★★★★★★★★★★★★

In 1955, two hurricanes, Connie and Diane, bore down on the eastern seaboard in a fury. In the Poconos Mountains of western Pennsylvania, Brodhead Creek, a 21.9-mile-long (35.2 km) tributary of the Delaware River, rose 30 feet (9.1 m) in 15 minutes, killing nearly 100 people. The flooding was so intense that houses floated down the Delaware River.

To prevent such damage from happening again, Congress approved a takeover of thousands of acres of land, removing 600 families from their homes, to build a multipurpose dam across the Delaware River at Tocks Island. The plan was to create a 37-mile-long (59.5 km) and one-mile-wide (1.6 km) reservoir to provide flood control, water supply, and hydroelectric power, as well as to create the infrastructure for a new national recreation area that would skirt the man-made lake.

There was opposition to the project from the start. The Delaware River Basin Commission, a committee that included the governors of New Jersey, Pennsylvania, Delaware, and New York, voted against the dam in 1975 by a three-to-one margin. But efforts through 1977 to deauthorize the dam through Congress failed. In 1978,

SIZE OF PARK: 104.2 square miles (270.09 sq km) ★ BEST TIME TO GO: Year-round
YEAR ESTABLISHED: 1965 ★ IN-PARK ACCOMMODATIONS: Camping

Beautiful Dingmans Falls can be reached from a handicap-accessible trail in the park.

New Jersey may have the highest population density in the U.S., but it is nicknamed the Garden State for good reason. Seventy-four miles (119.1 km) of the 2,174-mile-long (3,498.7 km) Appalachian Trail run through N.J., and the highest, most beautiful portion follows Kittatinny Ridge (up to 1,803 feet/549.6 m) 24 miles (38.6 km) through the national recreation area.

however, the Middle Delaware was included in the Wild and Scenic Rivers Act, earning it designation as a Scenic and Recreational River. That was the final nail in the coffin for the dam. Development of that type wasn't allowed on a protected river. The U.S. Army Corps turned their lands over to the management of the National Park Service, and the dam was finally officially deauthorized in 1992.

Watch the sun set from overlooks on Mount Tammany.

Find historic buildings, like this old barn in Millbrook Village.

Easy paddling awaits for kayakers and canoers looking to spend a day on the river.

The result is a 70,000-acre (28,328 ha) park in New Jersey and Pennsylvania that encompasses 40 miles (64.4 km) of the Middle Delaware National Scenic River surrounded by 67,000 acres (27,113.9 ha) of forested mountains, river valleys, and floodplains. Close to some of the most densely packed urban areas in the country, the Delaware Water Gap offers river access in the form of boat launches, swimming beaches, and campsites for paddlers; and more than 150 miles (241.4 km) of hiking trails, 27 of which are part of the Appalachian Trail. Many of the trails lead to cascading waterfalls, mountain summits, or clear vistas of the park's most famous feature: the Delaware Water Gap. This 1,000-foot-deep (304.8 m) gap where the river slices through the Appalachian Mountains formed over millions of years. At river's edge, the opening is a half mile (0.8 km) wide. At the top, it's twice as wide, measuring a mile (1.6 km) between the Blue Mountains of Pennsylvania and Kittatinny Ridge on the New Jersey side. There are several vantage points in the park from which to view this arresting geologic formation. ■

CENTRAL PARK

★★★★★★★★★★★★★★★★★★★★★★★★★

In 1853, when state officials approved the funds to purchase land for a park in Manhattan, little did they know that this rocky, swampy terrain covered in small farms would one day become the beloved "lungs of the city" and a respite for 42 million annual visitors. As park designer Frederick Law Olmsted said about his vision for the park, it should be "a specimen of God's handiwork" that could be to common people "inexpensively, what a month or two in the White Mountains or the Adirondacks is, at great cost, to those in easier circumstances."

Olmsted and his British architect partner Calvert Vaux designed their "Greensward Plan," which allowed for formal and natural settings. The especially visionary element of the plan was their series of subterranean "transverse" roads, a feature that allowed pedestrians and carriages alike to enjoy the park without disturbing each other.

More than a century later, much of the original park infrastructure, such as the Bethesda Terrace, the Mall, the Lake, and the Pond, still exist. Some are vastly improved, like Hallett Nature Sanctuary.

The smallest of the park's woodland areas, the former Promontory, was closed to the public for more than 80 years after invasive species like Norway maple, black cherry, and Japanese knotgrass strangled the native foliage. In 2016, after five years of restoration by the Central Park Conservancy, Hallett reopened with a healthier landscape that is now an oasis for park wildlife. Central Park is one of the most visited parks in the country, and is a favorite destination for both residents and visitors to the city. ■

SIZE OF PARK: 1.31 square miles (3.41 sq km) ★ **BEST TIME TO GO:** Year-round
YEAR ESTABLISHED: 1858 ★ **IN-PARK ACCOMMODATIONS:** None

Central Park is surrounded by some of Manhattan's most iconic skyscrapers.

STATUE OF LIBERTY NATIONAL MONUMENT

★★★★★★★★★★★★★★★★★★★★★★★★★

Between 1892 and 1924, nearly 12 million immigrants would enter the United States through Ellis Island and the Port of New York and New Jersey. The Statue of Liberty National Monument honors the immigrants, who oftentimes traveled in crowded and unsanitary conditions seeking freedom and opportunity in the United States.

Standing erect on 12-acre (4.9 ha) Liberty Island, also part of the national monument, is the Statue of Liberty. France gifted it to the United States to commemorate the 100-year anniversary of the Declaration of Independence and to celebrate the friendship between the two countries.

Built in Paris by the sculptor Frédéric-Auguste Bartholdi, Lady Liberty had quite a journey of her own. Completed on a Paris rooftop in July 1884, the statue was broken down into 350 individual pieces and packed into 214 crates in order to ship it safely across the Atlantic on the frigate *Isère*.

The copper Green Goddess stands proudly atop a pedestal that rises nearly 10 stories—and 224 steps—from the ground. In an effort to raise funds for the pedestal, American poet Emma Lazarus wrote her iconic sonnet, "The New Colossus," in 1883. It includes these famous words carved on a plaque at the base of the statue.

"Give me your tired, your poor,
Your huddled masses yearning to breathe free,
The wretched refuse of your teeming shore.
Send these, the homeless, tempest-tost to me,
I lift my lamp beside the golden door!" ■

SIZE OF PARK: 39.5 acres (15.9 ha) ★ **BEST TIME TO GO:** Year-round
YEAR ESTABLISHED: 1924 ★ **IN-PARK ACCOMMODATIONS:** None

An American icon, the Statue of Liberty can be seen from the water on a ferry from Staten Island.

FLIGHT 93 NATIONAL MEMORIAL

★★★★★★★★★★★★★★★★★★★★★★★

On September 11, 2001, Capt. Jason M. Dahl carried his lucky talisman—a box of rocks from his son—on board United Airlines Flight 93, scheduled to depart Newark, New Jersey, at 8 a.m. Forty-six minutes into the flight to San Francisco, four hijackers broke into the cockpit and wrestled control from Dahl, turning the plane southeast on a path toward Washington, D.C.

At 9:57, flight attendants and passengers rushed the cockpit in an attempt to regain control. Six minutes later, the plane crashed in an open field in Somerset County. Without this heroic effort by the captives, Flight 93 would have arrived in Washington, D.C., 20 minutes later, ostensibly to crash into the White House or the Capitol building.

More than 1,000 local, state, and federal evidence recovery teams, directed by the FBI, sifted through the site to piece together the nearly unrecognizable wreckage. When the investigation was completed, they covered the crater and planted grass seed and wildflowers.

The site, now a memorial, is described by its design team Paul Murdoch Architects and Nelson Byrd Woltz Landscape Architects as "severe and serene." Honor the passengers and crew by visiting the 40 engraved marble panels of the Wall of Names, listening to the 40 wind chimes emanating from the 93-foot-tall (28.3 m) "Tower of Voices" sculpture, and reading about the horrific catastrophe and the subsequent investigation. ∎

SIZE OF PARK: 8.5 square miles (22 sq km) ★ BEST TIME TO GO: Year-round
YEAR ESTABLISHED: 2002 ★ IN-PARK ACCOMMODATIONS: None

Starting at the visitors center parking lot, the Flight Path Walkway passes through gaps in marble-clad walls and leads to a platform overlooking the crash site.

FORT ADAMS STATE PARK

★★★★★★★★★★★★★★★★★★★★★★★★

It once served as the largest coastal fortress in the United States, but today Fort Adams, which sticks out like a thumb into Newport Harbor, is more synonymous with rest and relaxation: It's the home base for Sail Newport, New England's largest public sailing center; the annual host of the world-renowned Newport Jazz and Folk Festivals; and a popular spot for picnickers, thanks to its ambling grounds and wide-open views to Newport Bridge and Narragansett Bay.

Construction on the fort began in 1834 and took more than three million dollars and three decades to complete. Built to be the largest coastal defense works of its kind in the United States, the fort was constructed from Maine granite, shale, and brick and, during wartime, was big enough to house up to 2,400 men who could mount attacks with 468 guns around a perimeter of more than 1,700 yards. An active post for many wars, Fort Adams' most crucial role was during World War II, when it protected Rhode Island, a center of manufacturing war machinery including Liberty ships, torpedo boats, torpedoes, and Johnson carbines, from attack.

The fort was deactivated in 1950 at the onset of the Korean War. But in the late 1950s, President Dwight D. Eisenhower used its large Victorian commanding officer's residence as his summer White House. He liked its proximity to the golf course at Newport Country Club. ■

SIZE OF PARK: .31 square mile (.08 sq km) ★ BEST TIME TO GO: Year-round
YEAR ESTABLISHED: 1965 ★ IN-PARK ACCOMMODATIONS: None

Fort Adams was established on July 4, 1799, as a U.S. Army post.

MARSH-BILLINGS-ROCKEFELLER NATIONAL HISTORICAL PARK

★ ★

This small swath of forest and farm nestled in the rolling green hills of east-central Vermont may be a mere speck on a map compared to Yosemite or Yellowstone, but it plays a crucial role in the National Park Service as the only park in the system devoted to telling the evolving story of land conservation and stewardship in the United States.

The park, which consists of a brick-red 1805 Queen Anne–style mansion, surrounded by forest, was home to three important figures: First, George Perkins Marsh, who wrote *Man and Nature,* considered the founding text of America's conservation movement. In 1869, Frederick Billings bought the Marsh family farm and surrounding property and created the country's first sustainably managed forest. His granddaughter, Mary French Rockefeller, inherited the property in 1951.

Her husband, Laurance, played a key role in conservation movements across the U.S., including creating Virgin Islands National Park in the 1950s. In 1992, the couple donated the home, and 555 acres (224.6 ha) on neighboring Mount Tom, to the National Park Service.

The park, in conjunction with the Woodstock Foundation, built the Forest Center, a LEED-certified sustainable classroom and meeting space, to continue the work of these visionaries. ∎

SIZE OF PARK: 1 square mile (2.5 sq km) ★ **BEST TIME TO GO:** May to October
YEAR ESTABLISHED: 1992 ★ **IN-PARK ACCOMMODATIONS:** None

The historical park preserves Frederick Billings's land, established as a forest and progressive dairy farm.

SHENANDOAH NATIONAL PARK

★★★★★★★★★★★★★★★★★★★★★★★

From the time Yellowstone, the world's first national park, was established in 1872, it took almost another half century to establish Acadia, the first national park east of the Mississippi River. Sixteen years later Shenandoah National Park was created to protect a genteel Appalachian landscape full of cascading waterfalls, misty views of the Blue Ridge Mountains, fields of wildflowers, and wooded hollows that are home to deer, black bears, and songbirds.

The creation of the park, a move favored by politicians, tourism promoters, and conservationists, posed a fundamental problem: While it sat 75 miles (120.7 km) from Washington, D.C., and within a convenient day's drive of 40 million potential visitors, much of the land was private and occupied by mountain families, many of whom were tenants or squatters who did not want to leave their homes. These Appalachian mountaineers were summed up in a letter to park developers written by Miriam M. Sizer, an educator hired in the late 1920s to study the communities within the proposed park land in preparation for removing them:

"They are a modern Robinson Crusoe, without his knowledge of civilization," she wrote. "Steeped in ignorance, wrapped in self-satisfaction and complacency, possessed of little or no ambition, little sense of citizenship, little comprehension of law, or respect for law, these people present

SIZE OF PARK: 312 square miles (808 sq km) ★ BEST TIME TO GO: Year-round
YEAR ESTABLISHED: 1935 ★ IN-PARK ACCOMMODATIONS: Lodges & camping

Shenandoah National Park stretches out below overlooks accessed via hiking trails or from Skyline Drive.

a problem that demands and challenges the attention of thinking men and women."

To address this "problem," the government forced the resettlement of 500 families between 1935 and 1937. In an effort to relocate them, the Department of Agriculture's Resettlement Administration purchased 6,291 acres (2,545.9 ha) bordering the proposed park. By 1938, 42 elderly residents had been given life estates, 175 families had been

Two Mile Run Overlook leads past some of Shenandoah's most scenic stretches.

A young buck stands at alert within the forest.

A waterfall on the Staunton River flows along the Bear Church Rock trail.

relocated to the resettlement communities, and several families had been evicted, their houses burned down after their departure. Most of the mountain residents, however, left by their own accord. The families' forced eviction and the new park's subsequent development of separate-but-unequal facilities for Black visitors are reflective of the many difficult chapters in the development of the nation's national parks.

After Shenandoah was established in the 1930s, it swiftly became a hot attraction, especially for motorists touring the brand-new 105-mile-long (169 km) Skyline Drive with its mountain laurels and gauzy mountain views. Today, 40 percent of the park, almost 80,000 acres (32,374 ha), is a congressionally designated wilderness, where visitors can enjoy the park's hills and hollows in solitude. Rock climbers flock to the rock scrambles and panoramic views on routes along the 3,284-foot (1,001 m) granite Old Rag, while hikers prefer the 9.4-mile (15.1 km) round-trip path to its summit. ■

GEORGE WASHINGTON'S MOUNT VERNON

★ ★

Among his many qualities, the first president of the United States was a terrific dancer, the greatest horseman of his time, and so social that he and his wife, Martha, dined alone only twice in the last 20 years of their marriage. In addition to his legendary status as a general and farmer, George Washington owned one of the largest whiskey distilleries in the colonies. These are just a few pieces of history visitors learn as they wander the house and grounds of Washington's sprawling 8,000-acre (3,237.5 ha) estate.

The dark side of the ingenious farmer and war hero, however, was that, at the time of his death, 317 men, women, and children were enslaved at Mount Vernon. To understand how they lived and were treated, take the hour-long Enslaved People of Mount Vernon Tour, which has been on offer since 1994. See the enslaved peoples' quarters and their few possessions. More important, hear their personal stories from 50-year-old field worker Caesar, who was literate and preached the Bible, to Washington's valet Christopher Sheels, who was instructed to wear his long hair pulled back in a "queue" in the manner of the gentlemen of the day. After the tour, ponder the nation's complicated history from the back veranda overlooking the Potomac River. Its placid viewshed has been preserved to look exactly the same as the one Washington had in his day. ■

SIZE OF PARK: 0.6 square mile (1.5 sq km) ★ **BEST TIME TO GO:** Spring & fall
YEAR ESTABLISHED: 1758 ★ **IN-PARK ACCOMMODATIONS:** None

Just 13 miles (20.9 km) from the nation's capital, Mount Vernon preserves the home of the first U.S. president.

NATIONAL MALL AND MEMORIAL PARKS

★★★★★★★★★★★★★★★★★★★★★★★★

There is a lot to unpack in "America's Front Yard," the nickname for the more than 1,000 acres (404.7 ha) of green space that make up the National Mall and Memorial Parks in Washington, D.C., stretching from the foot of the U.S. Capitol to the Potomac River and from the White House to the Jefferson Memorial. In total, the park encompasses more than 100 unique monuments, memorials, statues, fountains, and more, some of which lie in greater D.C.

Every year, the park receives more than 25 million visitors, a number larger than the annual visitation of Yellowstone, Yosemite, and Grand Canyon National Parks combined.

Where to start? That's a visitor's most difficult question. Perhaps the best way to begin is to download the D.C. Area National Parks app and determine which of the National Mall's eight major memorials most speak to you. Another good way to start is to take an elevator to the viewing platform of the Washington Monument. Since 1888, this 550-foot-tall (167.6 m) marble obelisk has honored George Washington, the father of the nation who led the Continental Army to victory over Great Britain, presided over the Constitutional Convention, and served as the first president of the United States.

At the Lincoln Memorial, guests can honor the nation's 16th president, who grew up so poor in a Kentucky cabin that one neighbor described it as

---

SIZE OF PARK: 10.12 square miles (26.23 sq km) ★ **BEST TIME TO GO:** Year-round
YEAR ESTABLISHED: 1965 ★ **IN-PARK ACCOMMODATIONS:** None

The Washington Monument was built in the 1800s to honor the president and military leader.

CULTURAL HIGHLIGHT

Since construction began on the Vietnam Veterans Memorial in 1982, visitors have left articles and personal memorabilia—photographs, sealed letters, a stuffed Santa Claus, a custom-built motorcycle, and other items—to commemorate the 58,000 U.S. soldiers who died or were unaccounted for at the time the wall was built. Since 1984, more than 400,000 of these items have been added to the parks' museum collection.

"a hunters hut not fit to be called home." Lincoln was so intelligent that he devoured books by candlelight and was so physically strong that he was nicknamed "the Rail Splitter." The memorial devoted to him is a grand facsimile of the temples built in ancient Greece. The backlit marble statue of the president was designed to showcase the immense achievements of this once poor farm boy who unified the nation after the Civil War.

More than 58,000 names are etched into the 200-foot-long (61 m) Vietnam Veterans Memorial, listed in chronological order by date of casualty.

The Lincoln Memorial stands at one end of the National Mall's iconic reflecting pool, the Washington Monument at the other.

> 66 All the monuments ... are a moving testament to the fact that the freedom we so value as Americans is never free. 99

All the monuments—from the Martin Luther King, Jr., Memorial to the Vietnam Veterans Memorial to the Korean War Veterans Memorial—are a moving testament to the fact that the freedom we so value as Americans is never free. It can be overwhelming to take in all of this intense history, which is why park designers included reflective pools, quiet gardens, and meditative spaces to contemplate the contributions and sacrifices so many Americans have made to the nation. ■

NEW RIVER GORGE NATIONAL PARK AND PRESERVE

★★★★★★★★★★★★★★★★★★★★★★★★★

The country's newest national park (designated in February 2021) contains 53 miles (85.3 km) of one of the oldest rivers on the planet. The 300- to 360-million-year-old New River is so ancient that the Appalachian Mountains rose up around it as its water simultaneously cut through the bedrock. The result is the deepest and longest river gorge in the Appalachians where, at one point, the elevation from the river's edge to the rim is 1,400 feet (426.7 m).

This undammed river freely flows north through one of the oldest and most diverse ecosystems in the world, providing refuge for 46 species of native fish, birds such as colorful and elusive wood-warblers and majestic peregrine falcons, and two federally endangered mammals—the Indiana and Virginia big-eared bats.

This rugged, wild portion of the Appalachians feels almost untouched. And it mostly was until 1873, when new railroad tracks opened up the region to coal mining and timber harvesting. Throughout the park, visitors can find the remains of the railroad and even visit the former boomtown district of Thurmond, which, during its

SIZE OF PARK: 113.7 square miles (294.64 sq km) ★ **BEST TIME TO GO:** April to October
YEAR ESTABLISHED: 2020 ★ **IN-PARK ACCOMMODATIONS:** Camping

Rafting is a must-do in the nation's newest national park.

In the 1890s, when the local regional hospital refused to serve those infected with smallpox, the town of Red Ash built two "pest houses"—one for men and one for women and children—on the 12-acre (4.9 ha) island of Red Ash in the New River. The island was used for the same purpose during the 1918 influenza epidemic.

heyday, generated the most freight revenue on the C&O Railway. Its restored 1904 depot is seasonally open to the public.

Most visitors come to the New River Gorge to immerse themselves in the refreshing water. Fishermen line the banks or float the mellower sections of the New, casting for walleye, muskie, crappie, bluegill, catfish, and several species of bass. For

Grandview overlook offers one of the best panoramas of the New River Gorge, especially during sunrise and sunset.

The New River Gorge Bridge is reflected in the calm water below.

Castle Rock and Grandview Rim Trails form a one-mile (1.6 km) loop.

decades, expert whitewater paddlers have tested their skills on the New River's Lower Gorge, which offers some of the most challenging technical whitewater in the country, with rapids ranging from intermediate Class III to the most extreme Class V. Less experienced paddlers can sign on with one of a number of licensed outfitters who run trips from April through October. The river is particularly stunning in the fall, when the gorge is flaming with crimson, yellow, and orange foliage.

For a more vicarious thrill, time a visit with Bridge Day, held annually on the third Saturday of October, when the New River Gorge Bridge, which spans the river near the town of Fayetteville, opens to pedestrians. Rising 876 feet (267 m) out of the Gorge, the bridge is the third-highest in the country. On this one day of the year, a 5K run starts on the bridge, people can rappel off, and hundreds of BASE jumpers fling themselves into the Gorge while spectators cheer them on. ■

PART FOUR

THE SOUTH

A bald cypress grows from the calm waters of the Atchafalaya Basin in Louisiana (p. 302).

SELMA TO MONTGOMERY NATIONAL HISTORIC TRAIL

★★★★★★★★★★★★★★★★★★★★★★★★★★★

"They told us we wouldn't get here. And there were those who said that we would get here only over their dead bodies, but all the world today knows that we are here and we are standing before the forces of power in the state of Alabama saying, 'We ain't goin' let nobody turn us around.'"

Martin Luther King, Jr., spoke these words to a crowd of 25,000 peaceful protestors on March 25, 1965, at the end of a tense five-day march from Selma to Montgomery. This 54-mile-long (86.9 km) journey is the foundation for the national historic trail, commemorating the three harrowing weeks that began on March 7 in Selma, where 600 nonviolent protestors set out for Montgomery to demand their constitutional right to vote. When they reached the Edmund Pettus Bridge, law enforcement officers attacked the marchers with billy clubs, tear gas, and horses. The news reports from Bloody Sunday transfixed the nation.

On March 21, more than 3,000 protestors once again set out toward Montgomery. This time state and federal law enforcement officers lined U.S. Highway 80 to ensure a peaceful march. The protestors grew to 25,000 by the time the march ended on the Capitol steps in Montgomery, where King delivered his famous speech, borrowing a line from Unitarian minister Theodore Parker: "How long?" King implored. "Not long, because the arc of the moral universe is long, but it bends toward justice." Five months later, on August 6, President Lyndon B. Johnson signed the Voting Rights Act into law. ■

SIZE OF PARK: 54 miles long (86 km) ★ BEST TIME TO GO: Year-round
YEAR ESTABLISHED: 1996 ★ IN-PARK ACCOMMODATIONS: None

The Edmund Pettus Bridge was the site of the brutal Bloody Sunday beatings of civil rights marchers.

BUFFALO NATIONAL RIVER

★ ★

The Buffalo River has the important distinction of being the United States' first national river, a designation that preserves its "outstanding natural, cultural, and recreational values in free-flowing condition for the enjoyment of present and future generations." Originating in the Boston Mountains of the Ozark Plateau, the undammed river meanders through the karst country of Newton, Searcy, and Marion Counties before it merges with the White River in Baxter County.

The 135-mile-long (217.3 km) national river portion, with its three designated wilderness units, dramatic limestone and sandstone bluffs, more than 500 caves, 100-plus miles (160.9 km) of hiking and horseback riding trails, and 12 species of game fish, is a beloved destination for paddlers, hikers, horseback riders, speleologists, anglers, and bow hunters.

Its national river designation did not come easily. In 1938, when Congress passed the Flood Control Act, a bill signed by President Franklin D. Roosevelt to authorize civil engineering projects like dams, dikes, and levees, the Army Corps of Engineers immediately began eyeballing the Buffalo's hydroelectric potential. They planned two dams, one in the middle section of the river, near the town of Gilbert, and one at the end near its mouth, as part of a larger dam project on the White River system.

By the early 1960s, the continued threat of a dam on the Buffalo River angered conservationists,

---

SIZE OF PARK: 147.3 square miles (381.5 sq km) ★ **BEST TIME TO GO:** Year-round
YEAR ESTABLISHED: 1972 ★ **IN-PARK ACCOMMODATIONS:** Lodges & camping

Follow the Buffalo
National River from above
along the Goat Trail.

The United States' first national river was established in 1972, protecting 135 miles (217.3 km) of the waterway.

who made speeches, brought media attention to the river, and pulled out the political red carpet, inviting Supreme Court justice William O. Douglas on a canoe trip down the Buffalo, an invitation he accepted. The debate finally came to a head in 1965, when Governor Orval Faubus refused to back the Corps of Engineers' plan to dam the waterway. Seven years later, Congress voted to establish it as the country's first national river.

Despite its protected status, the Buffalo is still vulnerable. In 2019, the nonprofit American Rivers ranked it as the eighth-most endangered river in the country due to the presence of a 6,500-head hog farm known as a concentrated animal feeding operation (CAFO) sitting on a hill above Big Creek, one of the river's main tributaries. The hog waste from the CAFO polluted groundwater wells and endangered the Buffalo River system, including critical habitat for threatened species like the rabbitsfoot mussel. In June 2019, the state reached an agreement with the hog farm to close the facility and Governor Asa Hutchinson announced a permanent moratorium on industrial-scale farms operating in the watershed. ∎

CONSERVATION HIGHLIGHT

The Buffalo's national river designation protects it from industrial uses, impoundments, and other obstructions that would alter the natural character of the waterway. Today there are 100 miles (20,438.7 km) of wild, scenic, and recreational rivers across the country, inclusive of 209 protected rivers in 40 states and Puerto Rico.

HOT SPRINGS NATIONAL PARK

★★★★★★★★★★★★★★★★★★★★★★★★★

Native tribes have been using the healing waters of what is now Hot Springs National Park for centuries, but it wasn't until the 1800s that Hot Springs became an American spa destination, attracting people from miles around to "quaff the elixir" in hopes of healing whatever ailments afflicted them. Today this unique national park nestled in the Ouachita Mountains protects the original outdoor thermal springs and an entire urban area with nine opulent historic bathhouses.

The water is deserving of reverence. It has made a long, hot journey to arrive here, starting 4,400 years ago, when precipitation fell on the surrounding 400-million-year-old Ouachita Mountains. The mountains' cracks and fissures formed a route that allowed the rainwater to travel 6,000 to 8,000 feet (1,828.8–2,438.4 m) below the earth's surface, slowly heating up the lower it went. As it hit the fault line deep below the earth's surface, it switched direction, traveling upward and bubbling out in Hot Springs along the historic Bathhouse Row.

One fascinating stop that elicits the glamour of the iconic town's heyday is the Fordyce Bathhouse, which now serves as a visitors center, but was the most opulent spa in town from 1915 to 1962. Its gymnasium, the precursor to a modern-day workout center, has a pommel horse, wooden "lifting clubs," and ropes that take their wiry climbers straight into the rafters. ■

SIZE OF PARK: 8.5 square miles (13.6 sq km) ★ **BEST TIME TO GO:** Year-round
YEAR ESTABLISHED: 1921 ★ **IN-PARK ACCOMMODATIONS:** Lodges & camping

Hot Water Cascade—the largest visible hot spring in the park—flows into two pools.

BISCAYNE NATIONAL PARK

★★★★★★★★★★★★★★★★★★★★★★★★

"**N**o sea-lover could look unmoved on the blue rollers of the Gulf Stream and the crystal-clear waters of the reef, of every delicate shade of blue and green, and tinged with every color of the spectrum ... a sort of liquid light, rather than water, so limpid and brilliant it is." Commodore Ralph Munroe, a native New Yorker, yacht builder, and founder of the Biscayne Bay Yacht Club, wrote these words in 1877 as a young man of 26.

It was the year after he purchased 40 acres (16.2 ha) on Biscayne Bay for $400 cash (plus a $400 yacht thrown in) to build his whimsical bungalow "the Barnacle," which, today, is the oldest house in Miami-Dade County.

In the nearly century and a half since Munroe wrote those words, the seventh-largest metropolitan area in the country has sprawled along Biscayne Bay. But the allure of its water remains as strong as it was in Munroe's day. Just south of Miami, Biscayne National Park is at the nexus of four ecosystems: southern Biscayne Bay, the mainland's mangrove forest, the northernmost Florida Keys, and a section of the third-largest coral reef in the world. Because of these four diverse ecosystems, Biscayne National Park contains more native fish species (more than 600) than all the fish, bird, reptile, amphibian, and mammal species combined in Yellowstone National Park.

SIZE OF PARK: 270 square miles (699 sq km) ★ **BEST TIME TO GO:** Year-round
YEAR ESTABLISHED: 1968 ★ **IN-PARK ACCOMMODATIONS:** Camping

The Boca Chita Key Lighthouse overlooks Biscayne Bay from a palm-tree-studded shoreline.

One needs access to a boat to experience the full beauty of this glorious water world. Biscayne National Park Institute, a unique partnership between the national park and the nonprofit Florida National Parks Association, offers ample opportunities to get out on the water. Visitors can sail with a captain on a 40-foot (12.2 m) boat to Elliott Key, the largest island in the park. On

Stroll through the park's bayfront on well-maintained boardwalks overlooking the Miami waters.

Elliott Key, hike the seven-mile-long (11.3 km) trail known as "the Spite Highway" or paddleboard through the peaceful mangroves of Jones Lagoon between Totten and Old Rhodes Keys, where the water is shallow and calm and the bottom is covered in lacy *Cassiopea* jellyfish, sea cucumbers, and sea stars. Snorkelers and divers will want to follow the Maritime Heritage Trail, which includes six shipwreck sites scattered throughout the park, including the *Mandalay,* a 112-foot (34.1 m) double-masted schooner that ran aground on New Year's Day in 1966. Above water, 130-feet-high (39.6 m) Fowey Rocks Lighthouse, first lit in 1878, shines over the bay as "the eye of Miami."

Layered on top of its natural beauty is the park's fascinating human history, which began 10,000 years ago, as evidenced by human bones found among the mammoth and condor remains at the Cutler Fossil Site. In more recent history, Biscayne Bay has also been a favorite of rum runners, pirates, pineapple farmers, billionaire yachties, and immigrants en route to a better life in the United States.

White ibises stand in the low-tide seagrass of the park.

HISTORICAL FOOTNOTE

The Jones Family Historic District marks the plot on Porgy Key that a Black man named Israel Lafayette "Parson" Jones bought for $300 in 1897. The family farmed pineapples and key limes and expanded to Totten Key, the site of a 250-acre (101.2 ha) pineapple plantation. Their success was tremendous for a southern Black family of that era. In 1992, Hurricane Andrew wiped out the farms and Jones's son Lancelot sold the property to the National Park Service for $1.2 million.

One of the more colorful sites in the park is Stiltsville, a community of over-water buildings, three-quarters of a mile (1.2 km) south of Key Biscayne that sprung up in the 1930s when "Crawfish" Eddie Walker, an entrepreneurial soul, built the first shack and started selling lobster chowder out of it. The ensuing years have yielded many legends of illegal alcohol running and gambling at Stiltsville. Today six buildings remain, all of which miraculously survived a battering by Hurricane Irma. ■

Biscayne boasts as much scenery under its waters as it does on dry land.

DRY TORTUGAS NATIONAL PARK

★★★★★★★★★★★★★★★★★★★★★★★

Halfway to Cuba, 70 miles (112.7 km) west of Key West, Florida, this tiny archipelago of seven sandy, tropical keys plays an important role in United States history. In 1846, the U.S. Army began constructing Fort Jefferson, a hexagonal fortress on Garden Key. The fort, built from 16 million handmade bricks and sprawling across 16 acres (6.5 ha), was to play a crucial role in protecting the southern coastline from invasion and suppressing rampant piracy in the Caribbean.

At its peak, Fort Jefferson housed 1,729 military personnel and was the third-largest fort in the country—but it was never fully completed or armed. During the Civil War, it became a prison for Union deserters, and later, civilians like Samuel Mudd, the physician convicted of conspiring with John Wilkes Booth to assassinate President Abraham Lincoln. By 1874, frequent hurricanes and yellow fever outbreaks forced the Army to abandon the fort.

Surrounding the fort is the cerulean water of the Gulf of Mexico and the terminus of the Florida reef system, the third-largest coral reef in the world. Visitors can snorkel right off the beach in clear seas among soft corals, nurse sharks, and rainbow-colored reef fish. In the summer months, the islands' namesake *tortugas,* or turtles, are seemingly everywhere. The national park is the most active nesting site in the Florida Keys for endangered green and loggerhead turtles. ∎

SIZE OF PARK: .22 square mile (.57 sq km) ★ **BEST TIME TO GO:** Year-round
YEAR ESTABLISHED: 1992 ★ **IN-PARK ACCOMMODATIONS:** Camping

Fort Jefferson stands strong, a centerpiece of Dry Tortugas.

EVERGLADES NATIONAL PARK

★★★★★★★★★★★★★★★★★★★★★★★★

In his 1947 dedication speech, President Harry S. Truman eloquently summed up Everglades National Park: "Here are no lofty peaks seeking the sky, no mighty glaciers or rushing streams wearing away the uplifted land. Here is land, tranquil in its quiet beauty ... To its natural abundance we owe the spectacular plant and animal life that distinguishes this place from all others in our country."

This fresh- and saltwater universe at the southernmost tip of Florida is the largest subtropical wilderness in the United States and contains such biodiversity that it is one of the only places in the world designated as a UNESCO World Heritage site, a Wetland of International Importance, *and* an international biosphere reserve. It's also the only place in the world to find both American crocodiles and alligators. The list of other residents includes 350 bird species, the West Indian manatee, schools of dolphins, and the endangered Florida panther, whose numbers have recently increased thanks to conservation initiatives by the park and its partners.

One of the most exciting ways to see the wildlife—and to add birds like the great blue heron, American wood stork, snail kite, purple gallinule, and roseate spoonbill to your life list—is to kayak or canoe the 99-mile (159.3 km) wilderness waterway between Everglades City and Flamingo. In the 7- to 10-day paddling journey through mazes of saltwater marshes and mangrove estuaries, and

SIZE OF PARK: 1,542,526 acres (624,238 ha) ★ BEST TIME TO GO: Year-round
YEAR ESTABLISHED: 1947 ★ IN-PARK ACCOMMODATIONS: Camping

Everglades National Park
preserves 1.5 million acres
(624,238 ha) of wetlands.

The Florida Fish and Wildlife Conservation Commission has found an innovative way to eradicate Burmese pythons. Every year, it hosts an annual Florida Python Challenge competition. The January 2020 event had 750 registered participants from 20 states who captured more than 80 pythons. If laid end to end, the snakes would have extended 647 feet (197.2 m).

up the mouths of freshwater rivers, paddlers can camp on wooden platforms raised above the water, known as chikees, or find a secluded coastal sand-beach site and build a campfire below the high-tide line. Don't forget a fly rod. The Everglades is one of the best places on the planet to fish for tarpon, snook, redfish, bonefish, and large-mouth bass.

Make the Long Pine Key Campground home for a weekend getaway among slash pines in the Everglades.

A young alligator, not an uncommon sight within the park, rests on a floating log.

Like many national parks today, the Everglades face serious conservation challenges. Climate-change-induced sea-level rise is transforming coastal marshes into brackish saltwater environments, endangering plants and animals like the federally protected Cape Sable seaside sparrow. Concerning invasive species, like the Burmese python, a vicious predator with razor sharp teeth that can grow up to 23 feet (7 m) long, have decimated animal populations like marsh rabbits, raccoons, opossums, and foxes. The good news is that the park is closely monitoring these issues and is working directly with state and federal agencies to control them. ■

66 This fresh- and saltwater universe ... is the largest subtropical wilderness in the United States. 99

MARTIN LUTHER KING, JR. NATIONAL HISTORICAL PARK

★★★★★★★★★★★★★★★★★★★★★★★★★

The powerful words and actions of Martin Luther King, Jr., have echoed through time. But who was this visionary from Atlanta and how did he become a Nobel Prize-winning civil rights leader before he was assassinated at the age of 39 on the balcony of a Memphis motel in 1968? Those are two questions Martin Luther King, Jr. National Historical Park sets out to answer.

Centered around a few city blocks on Auburn Avenue—the once thriving heart of Atlanta's Black community known as Sweet Auburn—the park highlights the most formative spaces in the young King's life, including his childhood home and Ebenezer Baptist Church, where King gave his first sermon at the age of 19. The park also features places like Fire Station No. 6, the first station in Atlanta to hire Black firefighters; the King Center, the final resting place of King and his wife, Coretta Scott King; an International World Peace Rose Garden, one of five throughout the world; and the "Behold" monument, a sculpture by Patrick Morelli commissioned by Coretta Scott King to commemorate the principles that guided the life and work of her husband.

SIZE OF PARK: .05 square mile (.14 sq km) ★ BEST TIME TO GO: Year-round
YEAR ESTABLISHED: 1980 ★ IN-PARK ACCOMMODATIONS: None

A statue of Kunta Kinte, from the novel *Roots*, stands at the entrance of the Ebenezer Baptist Church memorial center.

From the day he was born until the age of 12, King lived at 501 Auburn Avenue in an 1895 two-story Queen Anne–style house that his maternal grandfather, Reverend Adam Daniel Williams, bought for $3,500 from its white owners in 1909. The two-story house, with intricate scroll-cut wood trim and a front porch, was a bustling place: King shared the house with his

The International Civil Rights Walk of Fame

An eternal flame conveys the continued work toward King's dream.

The historical park is also the final resting place for Dr. Martin Luther King, Jr., and his wife, Coretta Scott King.

grandparents, parents, two siblings, and an occasional border.

Ebenezer Baptist Church, just down the block from King's childhood home, was perhaps the most influential space in his life. His grandfather became the church's pioneering second pastor in 1894, preaching a social gospel of Black business development and civil rights. When he died in 1931, King's father, Michael, or "Daddy King," a powerful patriarch and fierce preacher, became the head pastor. King, Jr., joined his father as co-pastor in 1959 and served at the church until his death. Of Ebenezer, King, Jr., once said, "My best friends were in Sunday School, and it was the Sunday School that helped me to build the capacity for getting along with people."

His last sermon at Ebenezer, delivered two months to the day before he was assassinated, "The Drum Major Instinct," powerfully articulated the dual imperatives of faith and citizenship. ∎

❝ His last sermon … powerfully articulated the dual imperatives of faith and citizenship. ❞

CUMBERLAND ISLAND NATIONAL SEASHORE

★★★★★★★★★★★★★★★★★★★★★★★★★

The shifting sand dunes, salt marshes, maritime forests, and miles of unspoiled beaches of Cumberland Island National Seashore on Georgia's largest and southernmost barrier island echo with ghosts from the past. From time immemorial, people have inhabited this 18-mile-long (29 km) island, from its original Indigenous residents to the Timucua people and Spanish missionaries to formerly enslaved Blacks to wealthy industrialists.

The wildly varied human history, juxtaposed with what is now a wilderness where wild turkeys, armadillos, and feral horses run free, is what makes a visit to this national seashore such a fascinating journey.

Accessible from the mainland town of St. Mary's via a 45-minute ferry, private boat, or kayak, guests arrive at Sea Camp, the visitors center on the southern end of the island. A short hike over to the Atlantic Ocean offers total solitude on 17 miles (27.4 km) of beach uninterrupted by man-made structures.

A mile (1.6 km) south of Sea Camp is Dungeness, what is left of one of many mansions on the island built by the Carnegie family. Constructed in 1884, the Queen Anne shingle-style home was meant to be used as the winter home of Thomas Carnegie, the younger brother and business partner of Andrew. Thomas died shortly after the house was finished, but his wife, Lucy, continued

---

SIZE OF PARK: 57 square miles (147 sq km) ★ **BEST TIME TO GO:** Year-round
YEAR ESTABLISHED: 1972 ★ **IN-PARK ACCOMMODATIONS:** Camping

Hiking trails lead through groves of plants and oak trees.

to expand and remodel the original structure to a massive 35,000 square feet (3,251.6 sq m) by the time she died in 1916. Decades later, in 1959, the mansion caught on fire and was left in ruins.

For a more intact perspective of what life was like for the very privileged of the late 19th century, rent a bike at Sea Camp and pedal the sandy road seven miles (11.3 km) north to Plum Orchard, a Georgian-style, 22,000-square-foot (2,043.9 sq m)

Cumberland Island is known for its wild horses, seen here grazing in front of the Dungeness mansion ruins.

The island is famous for its vast beaches and extensive trails, including wooden boardwalks around the seashore.

mansion built in 1898 for George Lauder Carnegie, a nephew of Andrew Carnegie. The fully intact home offers a glimpse into Edwardian high society, with an eclectic mix of period furnishings and reproduction items.

At the northern tip of the island, 15 miles (24.1 km) from where the ferry disembarks at Sea Camp, are the last remaining relics from the Settlement, a community established in the late 1800s by Black residents, some of whom were born into enslavement and freed after the Civil War. One of the last buildings standing is the one-room First African Baptist Church, built in 1893. It served an essential role in the community not only as a place of worship and fellowship, but also as a schoolhouse. ∎

66 From time immemorial, people have inhabited this 18-mile-long (29 km) island. 99

MAMMOTH CAVE NATIONAL PARK

★★★★★★★★★★★★★★★★★★★★★★★★★

Mapped at 420 miles (675.9 km) long, Mammoth is the longest known cave system in the world. With each new expedition, speleologists continue to find new passageways that are estimated to extend the system 600 miles (965.6 km) farther underground. Mammoth's 340-million-year-old limestone walls echo with fascinating human history that dates back more than 4,000 years, when prehistoric Native Americans mined its upper three levels six miles (9.7 km) deep in search of minerals like gypsum, selenite, mirabilite, and epsomite.

It is still a mystery how the ancient people used these precariously procured substances. Some clues can be found in the gourd bowls, pottery, woven cloth, and a few petroglyphs they left behind. Experts believe the petroglyphs, mostly geometric illustrations of humans, depict altered states of consciousness. In the 1930s, a desiccated corpse was found crushed under a six-ton boulder. A digging stick nearby indicated that the prehistoric man it belonged to had been mining gypsum when he died.

Legend has it that the cave was rediscovered at the turn of the 19th century, when a Kentucky homesteader named John Houchin shot and wounded a bear, then followed it into the cave entrance, the same one used by visitors today. The fate of the bear remains unknown, but the rediscovery of the cave was an economic boon to

SIZE OF PARK: 82 square miles (213.8 sq km) ★ **BEST TIME TO GO:** Winter & summer
YEAR ESTABLISHED: 1941 ★ **IN-PARK ACCOMMODATIONS:** Lodges & camping

A lantern illuminates a passageway in the cave along the Historic Tour route.

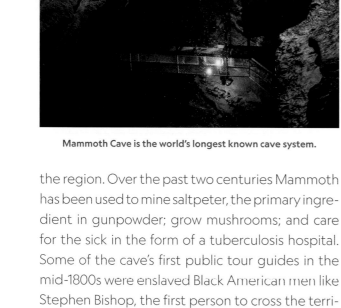

Mammoth Cave is the world's longest known cave system.

Greenery highlights an entrance to Mammoth Cave.

the region. Over the past two centuries Mammoth has been used to mine saltpeter, the primary ingredient in gunpowder; grow mushrooms; and care for the sick in the form of a tuberculosis hospital. Some of the cave's first public tour guides in the mid-1800s were enslaved Black American men like Stephen Bishop, the first person to cross the terrifying vertical shaft known as Bottomless Pit to discover miles of previously unmapped areas.

Today, guests can take ranger-led tours that last up to six hours. The most comprehensive and rigorous is the Wild Cave Tour, which turns visitors into amateur speleologists, crawling, climbing, and squeezing their way through a maze of small holes and canyons for five to six miles (8–9.7 km).

> ❝ Mammoth's 340-million-year-old limestone walls echo with fascinating human history. ❞

RARE SIGHTING

In 2019, researchers found fossilized 330-million-year-old shark teeth and cartilage in the cave walls that belonged to a species called *Saivodus striatus,* a common ctenacanth shark from the Late Mississippian age, approximately the size of a great white. The fossils represent a portion of geologic history that is not well represented in North America.

Aboveground, the park offers more than 85 miles (136.8 km) of hiking trails up and down rugged hills filled with leafy hardwood forests. The Green River, one of the most biodiverse waterways in the country, has ample sandy sidebars to stop at for a picnic lunch. Including riverside camping options, the park has a total of 13 designated backcountry sites, accessible via hiking or horseback. ■

In the Frozen Niagara section of the cave, calcium carbonate formations hang from the ceilings and walls.

ATCHAFALAYA NATIONAL HERITAGE AREA

★★★★★★★★★★★★★★★★★★★★★★★★★

More than a landscape, this heritage area in south-central Louisiana encompasses the rich and singular history and culture of the country's largest river swamp. This region known as the Atchafalaya Basin, which stretches across 14 of the state's 64 parishes, from Simmesport in central Louisiana 140 miles (225.3 km) south to the Gulf of Mexico, contains ancient oaks and towering cypresses along bayous, swamps, and backwater lakes, all centered around the Atchafalaya River, from the Choctaw words *hacha falaia,* or "long river."

Atchafalaya's surrounding basin—larger than the Everglades and containing the largest contiguous bottomland hardwood forest in North America—parallels the Mississippi River and acts as the primary floodway for Mississippi waters that need to be diverted from Baton Rouge and New Orleans.

This basin thrives with wildlife, from bobcats, black bears, and alligators, to 270 bird species, including the largest nesting concentration of bald eagles in the south-central United States. Its waters contain more than 100 species of fish and aquatic life, including delectable catfish, shrimp,

SIZE OF PARK: 10,400 square miles (26,935 sq km) ★ **BEST TIME TO GO:** Year-round
YEAR ESTABLISHED: 2006 ★ **IN-PARK ACCOMMODATIONS:** Lodges & camping

Tupelo trees, particularly suited for wet soils and flooding, stand tall in the Atchafalaya area.

HOT CUISINE

Gumbo is synonymous with Cajun country and is a metaphor for the melding of cultures that has taken place over centuries. It is derived from the word *nkombo,* Bantu for "okra," a vegetable the Portuguese originally brought to America. Another key ingredient is filé, which is Native American in origin and made from ground sassafras leaves. The dish's soup-like consistency is derived from a French bouillabaisse.

and crawfish, fundamental elements of the region's famed Cajun cuisine.

The cultural history of Atchafalaya is as complex as its waterways, starting 6,000 to 2,500 years ago, when the first Native Americans lived along natural levees and bayous of what was once the traditional Mississippi River floodplain. Starting in 1543 with Spaniard Hernando de Soto's expedition, Europeans started making forays into what

Paddle through the cypress swamps within the basin, a particularly colorful experience when scheduled in the fall.

You'll see plenty of ospreys nesting and flying throughout the heritage area.

is now Louisiana. During the 1700s, the French arrived in the Atchafalaya Basin to trade furs with its Indigenous inhabitants and launch raids into their tribal areas to capture and enslave people. Starting in 1703, roughly 3,000 Acadians from present-day Nova Scotia arrived after being exiled by the British. By 1718, most of the Native American population in the Atchafalaya had diminished as a result of diseases brought by the outsiders, as well as continuous warfare.

The Cajuns, descendants of the Acadians, are still the dominant culture in the Atchafalaya. But the region's food, music, and traditions have been heavily influenced by the Native American, Spanish, French, Caribbean, African, and Acadian people who have lived here over centuries. The Atchafalaya's racial and ethnic complexity is what makes it such a fascinating place to visit. It is, after all, "America's Foreign Country." ∎

66 This basin thrives with wildlife, from bobcats, black bears, and alligators, to 270 bird species. 99

GULF ISLANDS NATIONAL SEASHORE

★★★★★★★★★★★★★★★★★★★★★★★★★

Stretching 160 miles (257.5 km) from Florida's Santa Rosa Island in the east to Mississippi's Cat Island in the west, the nation's largest national seashore spans two states, includes seven islands and portions of the mainland, and has 13 unique areas, from historic forts that predate the Civil War to wilderness beaches of white quartz sand accessible only by boat.

Florida's Pensacola Bay, with its deep water and protected harbor, has long been considered the most important ship anchorage on the northern Gulf Coast. As such, it needed to be protected, and the U.S. began constructing forts along the coastline here in 1816. Fort Pickens, designed to protect the bay and the Pensacola Naval Yard, was purposely built to look massive and intimidating. On the west end of Santa Rosa Island, the fort could hold more than 200 cannons and unleash fire from a maximum of 1,000 soldiers when under a siege.

On the mainland, Fort Barrancas, the diamond-shaped "Bastion on the Bluffs" with its unobstructed view of the bay, was built with six million bricks in 1844 and also defended the Pensacola Navy Yard. The fort was so strategically positioned that it sat on the ruins of other strongholds built by the Spanish, French, and British as early as the 17th century. Built to stop foreign invasion, the only time the fort came under siege was during the Civil War.

On the Mississippi side of the islands, visitors can find solace among the seashore's salt marshes,

---

SIZE OF PARK: 215 square miles (556 sq km) ★ BEST TIME TO GO: September & October
YEAR ESTABLISHED: 1971 ★ IN-PARK ACCOMMODATIONS: Camping

Fort Barrancas is a monument to America's early defense systems.

The Davis Bayou Area offers several short hiking trails, a boat launch, and five picnic shelters.

sea-oat covered dunes, long stretches of white-sand beach, and forests of oak and pine. Two undeveloped barrier islands, Petit Bois and Horn, have additional protections as Gulf Islands Wilderness. Primitive backcountry camping is allowed at both for those with access to a private boat.

In many ways, Gulf Islands is a dreamy, idyllic destination, thriving with shorebirds and sea turtles and echoes of American history. A variety of animals make their nests and home there, including 12 threatened or endangered species, such as the Gulf sturgeon and West Indian manatee. But the seashore has also been under increasing human and climate-induced pressure: In 2010, the Deepwater Horizon spill resulted in gobs of oil and tar washing on the sand, resulting in a fishing and swimming ban. Intense hurricanes, most recently Zeta and Sally, have wreaked havoc on roads and infrastructure. The delicate dance between man and nature is fully on display across these islands. ■

HISTORICAL FOOTNOTE

Jim Crow laws in the South made many beaches off-limits to Black families. As a result, many Black children drowned because they swam in unsupervised or unsafe waters. To change these laws, Dr. Gilbert Mason, Sr., led peaceful "wade-ins," similar to restaurant "sit-ins," into Gulf of Mexico waters off beaches near Biloxi. Many of the protests were met with violence, but in 1968, the Justice Department finally prevailed in opening these public beaches to all.

CAPE HATTERAS NATIONAL SEASHORE

★★★★★★★★★★★★★★★★★★★★★★★★

Crashing surf, a solitary beach, and a cool dip in the Atlantic are what many visitors to North Carolina's Outer Banks seek. The three sandy islands—Bodie, Hatteras, and Ocracoke—parts of which make up Cape Hatteras National Seashore, offer this peaceful repose. They also provide refuge for five species of sea turtles, nesting colonies of shorebirds, and a herd of Banker ponies left by, as legend has it, shipwrecked sailors in the 16th or 17th century.

The history of the Outer Banks is a centuries-long string of harrowing tales of shipwreck and war. The water off the coast, known as the "Grave-yard of the Atlantic," has been the site of more than 600 shipwrecks, due to a "perfect storm" of deadly factors including the infamous Diamond Shoals, a bank of constantly shifting underwater sand extending eight miles (12.9 km) off the coast of Cape Hatteras; and two strong currents, the Labrador from the north and the Gulf Stream from the south, that converge to create a river of swiftly moving water. In order to take advantage of the currents, ships must sail close to the Outer Banks and risk the consequences.

The first recorded wreck was in June 1585, when Sir Richard Grenville's English ship, *The Tiger,* was heavily damaged in a storm while anchored off the coast. The unfortunate result was that the badly needed food and supplies for Roanoke colony were lost. Two centuries later, during the

SIZE OF PARK: 47 square miles (121.7 sq km) ★ **BEST TIME TO GO:** Year-round
YEAR ESTABLISHED: 1953 ★ **IN-PARK ACCOMMODATIONS:** Camping

The Bodie Island Lighthouse sits adjacent to a boardwalk that runs through Cape Hatteras.

Edward Teach, the pirate known as Blackbeard, terrorized the waters off the Outer Banks in the early 1700s. Ocracoke Inlet was Teach's favorite anchorage. On November 22, 2018, Teach was shot five times in battle with the British. The men of Lieutenant Robert Maynard threw his corpse into the inlet and his head was suspended from the bowsprit of their ship.

Civil War, the islands were used as battlefields. Whoever controlled them, and the surrounding sounds, would ultimately control North Carolina. By the summer of 1862, a Union victory on Roanoke Island secured eastern North Carolina for the north. Almost a century later, during World War II, German U-boats lurked offshore to wait for passing ships, illuminated by lights onshore. They

Surfers enjoy the waves in the Atlantic waters off the shores of the Outer Banks, particularly in the winter, when they are wilder.

Beach life in Cape Hatteras includes colorful cottages, available to book as vacation rentals.

torpedoed so many boats with this ambush technique that the region became known as Torpedo Alley. As recently as 2012, the *Bounty*, an enlarged reconstruction of its 1787 three-masted original, sank 90 miles (144.8 km) off Cape Hatteras during Hurricane Sandy.

To counter the perilous sea, many light stations were constructed along the Outer Banks, including the Cape Hatteras Lighthouse. At 198 feet (60.4 m), the iconic black-and-white-striped structure, designed and built between 1868 and 1870, is still the tallest brick light tower in the United States.

Visitors can kayak the calm, shallow waters of Roanoke and Pamlico Sounds, camp at one of four campgrounds within the park, take a dip in the Atlantic at one of its four lifeguarded beaches, or simply bask in the solitude of the national seashore with a long walk on the beach. ■

66 The history of the Outer Banks is a centuries-long string of harrowing tales of shipwreck and war. 99

WASHITA BATTLEFIELD

★★★★★★★★★★★★★★★★★★★★★★★★★

On November 27, 1868, Lt. Col. George Armstrong Custer led the Seventh U.S. Cavalry on a surprise winter attack on a Cheyenne village in Oklahoma Territory along the Washita River. The night before, Black Kettle, the respected village chief, had returned from a 100-mile-journey (160.9 km) in an effort to seek increased protection from the U.S. Army, a request that was refused.

Custer positioned four battalions around the sleeping Cheyenne camp, then led his battalion straight into Chief Black Kettle's village, while the other three attacked from the northeast and southwest. The Cheyenne were so outnumbered and caught off guard that few were able to return fire. It is estimated that between 16 and 140 men and up to 75 women and children died, including Chief Black Kettle and his wife, Medicine Woman Later, who were shot trying to cross the Washita River.

On December 14, the *New York Tribune* reported that "Colonel Wynkoop, agent for the Cheyenne and Arapahos Indians, has published his letter of resignation. He regards Gen. Custer's late fight as simply a massacre, and says that Black Kettle and his band, friendly Indians, were, when attacked, on their way to their reservation."

The Cheyenne are still working to change the name of the historic site 135 miles (225.4 km) east of Amarillo, Texas, to more accurately reflect the event that took place there. ∎

SIZE OF PARK: 12 square miles (31 sq km) ★ BEST TIME TO GO: Year-round
YEAR ESTABLISHED: 1996 ★ IN-PARK ACCOMMODATIONS: None

The Washita Battlefield commemorates the war between Chief Black Kettle and the U.S. Army.

CONGAREE NATIONAL PARK

★★★★★★★★★★★★★★★★★★★★★★★★

Prior to European settlement, the southeastern United States had more than 35 million acres (14.1 million ha) of floodplain forests. In South Carolina alone, the rivers were once bordered by more than a million acres (404,685.6 ha) of old-growth forests. Today only 12,000 acres (4,856.2 ha) remain, 11,000 (4,451.5 ha) of which are in Congaree National Park. This floodplain is the largest intact expanse of old-growth bottom-land forest remaining in the southeastern United States.

With an average canopy height of 130 feet (39.6 m), the trees here are comparable to ones found in old-growth forests across Japan, the Himalaya, southern South America, and Eastern Europe. Hikers and paddlers who immerse themselves in the forest here will find magnificent stands of towering bald cypress, water tupelo (large trees that live in deep rivers or coastal swamps), and the national champion loblolly pine, which soars 170 feet (51 m) into the sky.

The forest's health has everything to do with the floodplain in which it sits. The water from the Wateree and Congaree Rivers floods their banks and sweeps through this low-lying floodplain an average of 10 times per year. With its nourishing nutrients and sediments, the water rejuvenates the ecosystem, supporting forest growth in addition to an abundance of wildlife including river otters, deer, turtles, the occasional alligator, and 178 bird species.

SIZE OF PARK: 42 square miles (109 sq km) ★ **BEST TIME TO GO:** Year-round
YEAR ESTABLISHED: 2003 ★ **IN-PARK ACCOMMODATIONS:** Camping

Trees grow along the edge of Cedar Creek.

One man, Harry Hampton, is largely to thank for saving this floodplain forest from obliteration. Born, fittingly, in the town of Woodlands, Hampton became a journalist at the *State*, a daily paper based in Columbia founded by three of his uncles. For 34 years, between 1930 and 1964, Hampton wrote a column titled "Woods and Water" that focused on the outdoors and conservation—a

Congaree's canoe trail actually takes you through most of the park's federal wilderness.

A barred owl perches on a branch above the waters.

A skink, a type of lizard, climbs in a cypress swamp.

forward-thinking topic for that time. In the 1960s, Hampton started a campaign to protect the local forests from timber harvesting. His successful lobbying resulted in legislation that eventually established Congaree National Park. The visitors center is named in honor of the writer and conservationist who dedicated his entire career to preserving these majestic trees.

One of the best ways to experience the forest is to paddle a park waterway, like Cedar Creek, a portion of which winds through immense stands of bald cypress and towering tupelos draped with Spanish moss. Hikers can choose from more than 25 miles (40.2 km) of pathways, like seven-mile-long (11.3 km) Oakridge Trail that traverses a ridgeline of giant old oak trees and dips into low-lying sloughs, a favorite habitat for wild turkey. ■

66 Hikers and paddlers ... will find magnificent stands of towering bald cypress, water tupelo, ... and the national champion loblolly pine. 99

GREAT SMOKY MOUNTAINS NATIONAL PARK

★★★★★★★★★★★★★★★★★★★★★★★★★

Ten thousand years ago, at the end of the last ice age, these ancient mountains became a refuge for plants and animals that were displaced from farther north by the changing climate. As a result, Great Smoky Mountains contains the most biological diversity of any other national park in the United States. Scientists have been documenting the plants and animals here for more than a century.

Their current count is more than 20,000 species including 100 native trees, 1,500 flowering plants, 200 birds, and more than 9,000 insects.

The Cherokee, one of the most sophisticated tribes in North America, made their home here for centuries, living in towns governed by complex political systems and surrounded by cultivated farms, connected by an extensive network of trails. In the 1830s, pressured by settlers who wanted to grow cotton and other crops on land the Cherokee inhabited, the federal government forced them out, marching more than 125,000 people along the Trail of Tears, an oftentimes deadly journey west of the Mississippi River, where the government relocated them to "Indian Territory." Very few Cherokee remained behind, but

SIZE OF PARK: 816.2 square miles (2,113.9 sq km) ★ BEST TIME TO GO: Year-round
YEAR ESTABLISHED: 1934 ★ IN-PARK ACCOMMODATIONS: Lodges & camping

Catch a view of the Great
Smoky Mountains at its most
colorful time of day—dusk.

the ancestors of those who did still live outside the park boundaries today.

By the 1930s, timber companies had so aggressively razed the forests covering the slopes of the Smokies it soon became evident that if a park weren't created, very little wilderness would remain. A diverse group of conservationists played a part in the creation of the park, including

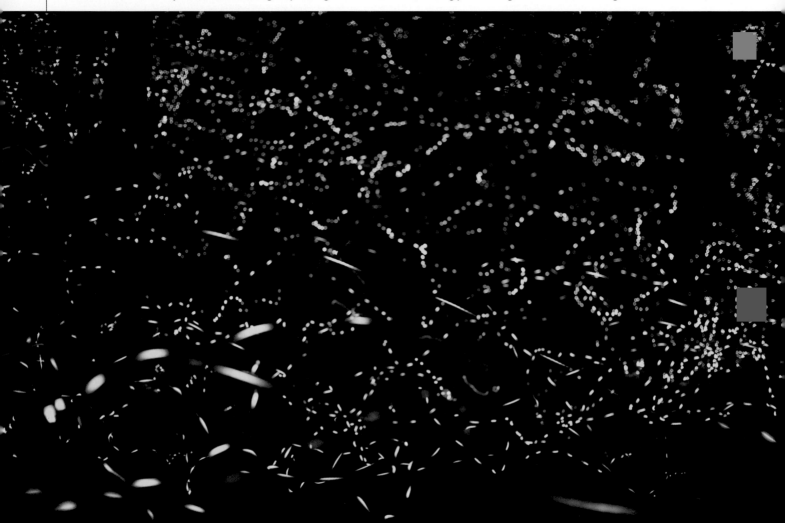

Synchronous fireflies light up the night within the forest, flashing yellow and green streaks in a mating ritual.

Though rare to see on a visit, black bears like this sleeping one do roam the park's acreage.

David Chapman, the influential president of a Knoxville drug company; George Masa, an immigrant from Japan who took beautiful photos of the Smoky Mountains; and Ann Davis, one of the first women elected to the Tennessee House of Representatives. By 1934, when the park was established, only 20 percent of the original forest within its boundary remained.

With more than 12 million visitors per year, Great Smoky Mountains is the most visited of all the U.S. national parks. And there are many ways for guests to experience its beauty. The crest of the Great Smokies runs for a continuous string of 36 miles (57.9 km) throughout the park. The highest point, 6,643-foot (2,024.8 m) Clingmans Dome, is also the highest point of the Appalachian Trail. From this vantage point, the 300-million-year-old mountains seem to roll on forever. ■

66 The crest of the Great Smokies runs for a continuous string of 36 miles (57.9 km) throughout the park. 99

GUADALUPE MOUNTAINS NATIONAL PARK

★★★★★★★★★★★★★★★★★★★★★★★★★

One of the least visited national parks, West Texas's Guadalupe Mountains emanate a powerful, subtle beauty throughout the Chihuahuan Desert landscape of canyons, dunes, and peaks. Known as "the Top of Texas," the state's four highest mountains can be found here, the tallest of which, Guadalupe Peak, is 8,751 feet (2,667.3 m).

But the park's most striking feature is El Capitan, a sheer 1,000-foot (304.8 m) cliff rising straight from the desert floor. It is part of the world's most extensive Permian fossil reef, a limestone formation created 260 million years ago by algae, sponges, and other invertebrate skeletons accumulated in the Delaware Sea that once covered most of western Texas and southwestern New Mexico.

It's hard to imagine permanently inhabiting this sparse landscape, but it was the final stronghold for the Mescalero Apache, who were driven to these mountains by their foes, the Comanche.

They survived by hunting elk, bighorn sheep, and mule deer, and also found multiple uses for the agave, or mescal, plant, cooking its hearts for sustenance and weaving its fiber into ropes, blankets, and sandals.

Guadalupe Mountains offers solitude, with 80 miles (128.7 km) of hiking trails and ample space to camp, stargaze, and bird-watch. There are more than 300 species that nest or migrate through here. One of the most beautiful times to visit the park is in the middle of October, when the brilliant yellows and reds of the bigtooth maple flare. ■

SIZE OF PARK: 135 square miles (350 sq km) ★ **BEST TIME TO GO:** Year-round
YEAR ESTABLISHED: 1972 ★ **IN-PARK ACCOMMODATIONS:** Camping

An open road runs through the natural monuments of Guadalupe Mountains National Park.

BIG BEND NATIONAL PARK

★★★★★★★★★★★★★★★★★★★★★★★★★

Big Bend National Park is an immense geologic puzzle. The sweeping Chihuahuan Desert landscape is the only place where the country's three major mountain-building episodes are pre-served and on display—from the southern terminus of the Rocky Mountains at Mariscal Mountain to the farthest extent of the basin and range to the hem of the skirt of the Appalachian Mountains in the north-ern part of the park south of Marathon, Texas.

Throughout the park, there are so many jum-bled rock formations, some exposed at odd angles and others seemingly displaced from where they currently sit, that geologists have spent decades trying to solve the great mystery of how they once fit together.

The landscape the geologic upheaval has cre-ated is fascinating to explore. With yawning, empty spaces, the park feels like one of the last untouched regions left in the lower 48. Yet humans have been exploring its rugged canyons, willow-lined river-banks, and desert mountains for 13,000 years. There are approximately 2,500 documented archaeolog-ical sites, including quarries where the Early Archaic people (8,000 to 1,000 B.C.) were pounding stone tools and arrowheads 10,000 years ago. Over the centuries, Big Bend was also home to the nomadic Chisos and Jumano people and the Comanche, who used the region as a base from which to make raids into interior Mexico until the mid-1800s.

SIZE OF PARK: 1,252 square miles (3,242.7 sq km) ★ **BEST TIME TO GO:** November to April
YEAR ESTABLISHED: 1944 ★ **IN-PARK ACCOMMODATIONS:** Lodges & camping

The Rio Grande cuts between Hot Springs and the Rio Grande Village.

A must-see of the park's nine National Register archaeological and historic sites is the Mariscal mine where, between 1900 and 1943, one quarter of the country's mercury was produced to create blasting caps and bomb detonators for both World Wars. The extraction of this valuable resource was destructive to the surrounding ecosystem because the miners cut down trees along

Called Balanced Rock for good reason, this formation is just one of many you can find throughout Big Bend.

the river, near the springs, and in the Chisos Mountains to fuel the furnaces to a temperature that would vaporize the mercury from the rock.

Even rangers who have worked in the park for decades still haven't discovered every nook and cranny of Big Bend. To do so would require lifetimes. To distill the park into one visit is almost impossible. But it's key to focus on a few major attractions: First is the awesome beauty of the well-preserved Chihuahuan Desert. This magical landscape of agave, century plants, and 45 of the world's 2,000 cactus species, seems to extend forever. The second is the Rio Grande, which starts in south-central Colorado and flows almost 2,000 miles (3,218.7 km) to the Gulf of Mexico. One hundred eighteen miles (189.9 km) of the Rio Grande comprises the park's southern border with Mexico. The river is the park's lifeblood and a multi-day trip down it will wend its way through one or more of the park's three impressive canyons, the most awe-inspiring of which is Santa Elena, with 1,500-foot (457.2 m) vertical limestone walls that jut straight up from the riverbank for miles. For a

Chisos agave grows wild on the land below the Chisos Mountains.

ROCK TALK

The geologic history on display at Big Bend ranges from 500-million-year-old rocks at Persimmon Gap to the sand dunes at Boquillas Canyon that shift whenever the wind blows. In between those two extremes are rocks that formed from sedimentation, fossilization, plate tectonics, erosion, and volcanism over millions of years.

sense of the park's immensity, spend a few nights in the backcountry hiking the Chisos Mountains' 14.4-mile (23.2 km) round-trip South Rim Trail. Time the hike to catch a sunset over Mexico from the top of the rim, then sleep under the Milky Way. In 2012, the International Dark-Sky Association awarded Big Bend Gold Tier status, meaning that it has a sky free from all but the most minor impacts of light pollution. The National Park Service later determined that it has the darkest night skies of any national park in the lower 48. ■

A rock formation glows, lit by the sunset over Big Bend.

PART FIVE

THE MIDWEST & THE PLAINS

The Lower Fox Creek
Schoolhouse in Tallgrass
Prairie National Preserve
in Kansas (p. 342)

GRANT PARK

★ ★

When the city of Chicago established Grant Park in 1835, there was one mandate: It would be "public ground forever to remain vacant of buildings." With the exception of a few important edifices like the Art Institute of Chicago museum campus, home to the Adler Planetarium, the Field Museum of Natural History, and Shedd Aquarium, that mandate has stuck.

"Chicago's Front Yard" remains a green oasis where its citizens can walk the shore of Lake Michigan, meander through gardens, play ball, and photograph the city's skyline reflected in "Cloud Gate," the 33-foot-high (10.1 m), 42-foot-wide (12.8 m) stainless steel work, nicknamed "The Bean," by Anish Kapoor.

Grant Park has also been an important national gathering place: In 1865, onlookers climbed lamp posts and trees to better glimpse assassinated President Abraham Lincoln's funeral procession. In 1968, it was the site of violent clashes between protestors and police during the Democratic Convention. In the 1990s, millions of Chicago Bulls fans, rejoicing in yet another NBA Championship victory, gathered to celebrate. After his sixth victory in eight years, Michael Jordan addressed the crowd for the last time in 1998: "No matter what happens, my heart, my soul and my love will still be in the city of Chicago," he told his adoring fans.

It's hard to top Jordan, but on November 4, 2008, President Barack Obama gave his victory speech in Grant Park, proclaiming to the crowd of 240,000 and the watching nation: "I will never forget who this victory truly belongs to. It belongs to you. It belongs to you." ■

SIZE OF PARK: .49 square mile (1.29 sq km) ★ BEST TIME TO GO: Year-round
YEAR ESTABLISHED: 1835 ★ IN-PARK ACCOMMODATIONS: None

A view from Grant Park of downtown Chicago, awash in the glow of golden hour

INDIANA DUNES NATIONAL PARK

★★★★★★★★★★★★★★★★★★★★★★★★

The struggle between development and preservation has never been more prevalent than on the southern tip of the Lake Michigan shoreline, where the steel mills and power plants of Gary and Michigan City, Indiana, sandwich the dune complexes and surrounding oak savannas, swamps, bogs, marshes, prairies, rivers, and forests that now make up Indiana Dunes National Park.

As early as the turn of the 20th century, important scientific research was taking place at the dunes. In 1899, Henry Chandler Cowles, the "father of plant ecology," published a journal paper, "Ecological Relations of the Vegetation on Sand Dunes of Lake Michigan." His work, however, wasn't enough to preserve the dunes. In 1916, the 200-foot (61 m) Hoosier Slide was shipped off to be melted into fruit jars and plate glass.

It took another half century before the dunes were officially preserved. In 1966, as part of an agreement known as the "Grand Bargain," Illinois senator Paul H. Douglas tirelessly worked to ensure that the Port of Indiana-Burns Harbor, a large industrial area and deep shipping channel, could only be established near the dunes if the sand in them was protected. The result was Indiana Dunes National Lakeshore, the precursor to the park, which protected 15 miles (24.1 km) of shoreline.

Indiana Dunes is fourth among U.S. national parks for its biodiversity, home to more than 1,100 plant species. ∎

SIZE OF PARK: 23.4 square miles (60.7 sq km) ★ **BEST TIME TO GO:** June to October
YEAR ESTABLISHED: 2019 ★ **IN-PARK ACCOMMODATIONS:** Camping

The Mount Baldy dune stands 126 feet (38.4 m) above Lake Michigan.

EFFIGY MOUNDS NATIONAL MONUMENT

★★★★★★★★★★★★★★★★★★★★★★★★★★

The U.S. once contained thousands of burial mounds. Built mostly east of the Mississippi River between 3500 B.C. and A.D. 1600, they were largely used for laying loved ones to rest or ceremonies. Roughly 1,000 years ago, the mounds became increasingly sophisticated. People known as the Effigy Moundbuilders, who inhabited what is now Wisconsin, Minnesota, Iowa, and Illinois, elevated the earthen structures to an art form, shaping animals and water spirits out of dirt.

Effigy Mounds National Monument on the western bank of the Mississippi River in the northeast corner of Iowa contains the largest surviving group of prehistoric mounds in the United States: 206 in total, 31 of which are in the form of a bird or a bear. The largest, Great Bear Mound, stretches 137 feet (42 m) from head to tail. From the air, the Marching Bear Group, comprising 10 bear-shaped mounds, appears to be walking in a line across the landscape.

During the 1950s and 1960s, the mounds were heavily excavated, destroying their historical value. In 1959, the national monument established a policy to prohibit further damage, allowing only nondestructive testing methods to be used. In the 1970s, the National Park Service shifted even further away from archaeological excavation, favoring cultural interpretation instead. That decision was bolstered by the 1990 passage of the Native American Graves Protection and

SIZE OF PARK: 3.77 square miles (9.78 sq km) ★ **BEST TIME TO GO:** May to October
YEAR ESTABLISHED: 1949 ★ **IN-PARK ACCOMMODATIONS:** None

From Fire Point, see the Mississippi River run between Effigy Mounds, in Iowa, and Wisconsin, to the left.

Emma Big Bear Holt died in 1968, but her spirit is still alive at Effigy Mounds, where she was the last remaining Ho-Chunk (Winnebago) to live a traditional lifestyle. In the summers, she built a wickiup, an oval hut made from grass, where she wove intricate baskets made from black ash. In the half century since she died, her baskets have become valuable collector's items.

Repatriation Act (NAGPRA), which required federal agencies and museums in possession of Native American human remains and cultural items to consult with lineal descendants and culturally affiliated tribes. In the case of Effigy Mounds, that meant consulting with the 20 American Indian tribes that are the living descendants of the Effigy Moundbuilders.

The Marching Bear mounds are composed of 10 bear-shaped mounds, first mapped in 1910.

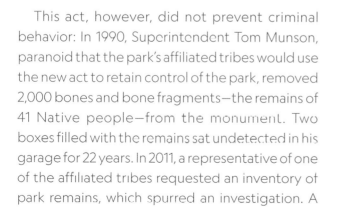

Mushrooms dot a tree in what is known as the Mysterious Forest.

A trail cuts through forest groves for easy hiking.

This act, however, did not prevent criminal behavior: In 1990, Superintendent Tom Munson, paranoid that the park's affiliated tribes would use the new act to retain control of the park, removed 2,000 bones and bone fragments—the remains of 41 Native people—from the monument. Two boxes filled with the remains sat undetected in his garage for 22 years. In 2011, a representative of one of the affiliated tribes requested an inventory of park remains, which spurred an investigation. A year later, a Park Service investigator solved the crime. Munson, who was 76, was sentenced to 10 weekends in prison, a year of home confinement, a $3,000 fine, and more than $100,000 in restitution. What is left of the remains have been returned to their respective tribes.

Park visitors can take a two-mile (3.2 km) guided tour along the park's Fire Point trail during the summer months that helps interpret these sacred, ancient monuments. ■

TALLGRASS PRAIRIE NATIONAL PRESERVE

★★★★★★★★★★★★★★★★★★★★★★★★★

Crashing oceans, desert canyons, and rocky summits often take precedence in the pantheon of iconic American landscapes, but one equally dramatic and often overlooked ecosystem is the subtle, powerful beauty of the tallgrass prairie. Historically, prairies covered 170 million acres (68.8 million ha) of North America, the waves of grass stretching from the Rocky Mountains to east of the Mississippi, and from Saskatchewan south to Texas.

The soil of these prairies, which began to appear 8,000 to 10,000 years ago, was too wet to become desert and too dry to maintain healthy forests. But it was perfect for creating one of the most complicated and diverse ecosystems in the world, second only to the rainforest of Brazil. Today, less than 4 percent of that prairie remains, most of which is preserved in the Flint Hills of Kansas between Wichita and Topeka.

The reason even this much prairie still exists today is that the limestone, shale, and chert of the Flint Hills made it very difficult for farmers to plow it under. As a result, its complex web of plant and animal life still thrives: 80 percent of prairie foliage is 40 to 60 species of Tallgrass. The remaining 20 percent consists of more than 300 species of flowers. There are few sites as stunning as a sea of sunflowers blooming under a moody Kansas sky in the middle of August. ■

SIZE OF PARK: 17 square miles (44.04 sq km) ★ BEST TIME TO GO: May to October
YEAR ESTABLISHED: 1996 ★ IN-PARK ACCOMMODATIONS: None

Dotted blazing stars add a burst of color to the brown tallgrass prairie.

ISLE ROYALE NATIONAL PARK

★★★★★★★★★★★★★★★★★★★★★★★★

A visit to the lower 48's most remote national park is like traveling in a time machine to a simpler era. The only way to access the car-free archipelago, which consists of one large 49-mile-long (78.9 km) island and 450 smaller islands that sit in the northwest portion of Lake Superior, is by ferry, private boat, or float plane. This extra layer of logistics adds excitement and suspense to the visit.

On the *Voyageur II*, an aluminum ferry that takes visitors from Grand Portage, Minnesota, 25 miles (40.2 km) to the park, the journey often begins in a thick mist rising from the frigid depths of the world's largest freshwater lake (by surface area). Two hours later, the boat arrives at the park's southwesternmost entrance, the Windigo ranger station, an outpost of a few seasonal cabins and a camp store that offers showers, laundry, and basic staples. Beyond those civilized amenities, there are 37 established campgrounds scattered across the island, a dense wilderness of boreal forest that is home to moose and wolves, and the settlement of Rock Harbor on the northeast coast. Because Isle Royale is so isolated, it has only 19 mammal species as compared to the 40 found on the surrounding mainland.

Alone on a footpath in such a remote wilderness, it's easy for visitors to feel as if they are the first to explore Isle Royale. But the island's human history dates back 4,500 years to the Indigenous

---

SIZE OF PARK: 850 square miles (2,201 sq km) ★ **BEST TIME TO GO:** Summer
YEAR ESTABLISHED: 1940 ★ **IN-PARK ACCOMMODATIONS:** Lodges & camping

A ranger house sits across a cove from Scoville Point in the park.

In 2019, the National Register of Historic Places designated Isle Royale National Park as "Minong Traditional Cultural Property." Numerous specific sites on the island were already registered for their European-immigrant history, but the new designation was in recognition of the entire archipelago's 4,500-year-old Ojibwe history.

descendants of the Ojibwe people, who called the archipelago Minong. The meaning of the word is believed to have originated from the words "Meen-oong," or "the good place," and describes a land where rich deposits of copper can be found. The Native Americans mined the metal to create knives, projectile points, ornaments, and even charms that they would keep

Hike the Indian Portage Trail from the West Chickenbone Lake Campground, a short but steep trek to the Greenstone Ridge.

in their medicine pouches to use as protection in battles and good luck in hunting bear and beaver. To extract the metal, resourceful miners would beat the bedrock with the rounded stones from the shores of Lake Superior. Ancient pottery and tools have been found at numerous sites throughout the national park.

The best way to explore the park's interior is via its network of backcountry hiking trails, the longest of which is the 40-mile (64.4 km) Greenstone Ridge Trail, which bisects the island, connecting the Windigo ranger station to Rock Harbor. The trail follows a low ridge through forests of white spruce, balsam fir, aspen, and birch trees to high points of exposed bedrock and inland lakes. Connecting trails take hikers to the shoreline of Lake Superior, where the Greenstone Trail's namesake gem, chlorastrolite, a semiprecious stone, can be found in the shoreline pebbles. While there are no campsites directly on the trail, short spur hikes lead to established camping areas, some of which have screened wooden shelters, a welcome respite from the plentiful mosquitoes.

While wolves are extremely elusive, it's not uncommon to see moose, the largest member of the deer family, while hiking. Keep a wide berth. The average moose is more than six feet (1.8 m) tall, weighs 1,000 pounds (453.6 kg), and can be aggressive. If their ears go up and the hair on the back of their neck stands erect, slowly back away and take a deep breath. ■

Bull moose can be seen grazing throughout Isle Royale.

WILDLIFE SIGHTING

Scientists have been studying the predator-prey relationship between wolves and moose on Isle Royale since 1958. In recent decades wolf populations have been nearly decimated due to disease and inbreeding, which has resulted in an overpopulation of moose, creating a dire threat to the island's ecosystem. In recent years 19 new wolves have been translocated to the island, in hopes of keeping the population of roughly 2,000 moose in check.

The Rock Harbor Light, closed
permanently in 1879, is the oldest
lighthouse within the park.

BOUNDARY WATERS CANOE AREA WILDERNESS

★ ★

To describe this northern Minnesota wilderness with 1,072 freshwater lakes surrounded by thick boreal forests as a "park" is a stretch. In reality, this rugged landscape bordering Canada's Quetico Provincial Park and inhabited by bald eagles, loons, moose, wolves, lynx, and black bears is a federally designated wilderness area that is so beloved, it sees an average of 155,000 visitors per year.

To accommodate their guests, the U.S. Forest Service maintains approximately 2,000 campsites with wilderness latrines and fire grates stretched across 1,200 canoe routes, which are lakes linked together via portages. While it's true that on the busiest summer weekends paddlers unfortunately may have to race each other to the last remaining campsite on the shoreline, it's also true that if you ski through the BWCAW in January, your only companions may be a pack of wolves howling under a full moon.

For centuries, paddlers have plied these waters, starting first with the Anishinabek—the forebearers of the Ojibwe (also known as Chippewa)—who still have their 1854 Treaty Authority to hunt, fish, and harvest wild rice in the BWCAW. In the 1600s, the French voyageurs pushed westward through this region from Lake Superior, searching for beaver pelts and a passage to the Pacific Ocean. Today, some of the most experienced living polar explorers, like Will Steger and Paul Schurke, who co-led the first unsupported dogsled journey to

---

SIZE OF PARK: 1,698 square miles (4,400 sq km) ★ **BEST TIME TO GO:** June to October, December to March
YEAR ESTABLISHED: 1978 ★ **IN-PARK ACCOMMODATIONS:** Camping

Paddle, portage, and camp
throughout the Boundary
Waters Canoe Area.

In 2020, the BWCAW was named an International Dark Sky Sanctuary, one of only 13 in the world. At more than one million acres (404,685.6 ha), the park is the largest of the sanctuaries. The naturally dark skies of northern Minnesota produce phenomenal displays of the flickering, emerald green aurora borealis, especially in the fall and winter.

the North Pole in 1986, still live on the edge of the wilderness and recreate within it because northern Minnesota's winter climate is the closest facsimile to the Arctic in the lower 48.

Most visitors, however, paddle these waters or hike the trails in the warm languorous days of summer, when the sun rises at 5 a.m. and sets at 9 p.m., leaving plenty of time to paddle and portage an

American beavers can be seen building and feeding throughout the area, if you have an eagle eye to spot them.

Water lilies cluster in a pond, surrounded by coniferous forest.

Pictographs on rock formations around North Hegman Lake

ambitious route with enough light left at the end of the day to find a campsite, set up tents, take a swim, and pick blueberries. It's always wise to build a few layover days into the schedule in case the walleye happen to be biting or the wind or thunderstorms make paddling too dangerous. Like in most beloved wild places, the increasing amount of human traffic has caused recent problems with trash, human waste, oversize or disruptive groups, and illegal cutting of trees. It is essential here to recreate responsibly by following leave-no-trace and tread-lightly principles, preventing search and rescues by recreating safely, and obtaining the proper travel permit and wilderness information before embarkment. ∎

66 The naturally dark skies of northern Minnesota produce phenomenal displays of the ... aurora borealis. 99

THEODORE WIRTH REGIONAL PARK

★ ★

In four out of six years between 2015 and 2021, the Trust for Public Land ranked Minneapolis the best city park system in the country, beating out close competitors like Washington, D.C. What sets Minneapolis's park system apart is that 98 percent of all residents—low, middle, and high income—live within a 10-minute walk of at least one city park.

There are 269 in total, which run like a green ribbon throughout the entire metro area, many connected by hiking and cycling paths and encompassing lakes, rivers, and gardens. The largest of them all is Theodore Wirth, a few miles west of downtown.

Named after a Swiss immigrant who held the position of Minneapolis parks superintendent for 29 years between 1906 and 1935, the densely wooded park is a model for the city's European-style park system. Slightly smaller than New York City's Central Park, it contains two golf courses, one lake, walking paths, and hiking trails, all amenities that might be expected in a city park.

More unique to Minnesota, however, is that this urban park is the epicenter of the city's thriving fat biking, mountain biking, cross-country skiing, and skijoring (dog-pulled cross-country skiing) scenes, with well-maintained, groomed trails for all these sports. Its trailhead adventure center rents bikes, skis, and snowshoes, and facilitates youth and adult programs for the widely diverse residents who rely on this beloved city resource. ∎

SIZE OF PARK: 1.18 square miles (3.07 sq km) ★ BEST TIME TO GO: Year-round
YEAR ESTABLISHED: 1889 ★ IN-PARK ACCOMMODATIONS: None

A swallowtail butterfly feeds on a purple wildflower during summer at the park.

VOYAGEURS NATIONAL PARK

★★★★★★★★★★★★★★★★★★★★★★★★★

Pack your swimsuit and a fishing rod. This rugged park that shares a 55-mile (88.5 km) border with Canada is one-third water, containing 80,000 acres (32,374.9 ha) of 30 clear freshwater lakes, surrounded by deep forests of white and red pine, spruce, and birch. Three of the park's four main bodies of water—the largest of which is 60-mile-long (96.6 km) Rainy Lake—surround the park's wild centerpiece, the 75,000-acre (30,351.4 ha) Kabetogama Peninsula.

This landscape of pillowy white pines and naked granite rock is home to deer, moose, beavers, bald eagles, and wolves, and contains 26 smaller inland lakes accessible from the mainland only by boat. Unlike most of the Boundary Waters Canoe Area Wilderness to the southeast, Voyageurs allows motors within its boundaries, so visitors can choose between the slow, peaceful pace of a kayak; the utilitarian appeal of a fishing boat from which to catch walleye, northern pike, and smallmouth bass; or the luxury of a houseboat to explore the park's 655 miles (1,054.1 km) of undeveloped coastline and more than 500 islands.

Voyageurs may seem distant and isolated from the population centers of the United States, but it was once a major crossroads for many Native cultures including the Cree, Monsoni, Assiniboine, and Ojibwe tribes. In the 1680s, French-Canadian voyageurs began traveling a 1,000-mile (1,609.3 km)

SIZE OF PARK: 341 square miles (883 sq km) ★ **BEST TIME TO GO:** Year-round
YEAR ESTABLISHED: 1975 ★ **IN-PARK ACCOMMODATIONS:** Lodges & camping

The sunset is reflected in shades of pink and orange on the waters of Mica Bay.

route between Lake Superior and Lake Athabasca, trapping beaver, muskrat, moose, and bear in order to feed the incessant demand for fur in the European fashion industry. They would stop at Kettle Falls, the natural barrier between Rainy and Namakan Lakes, to trade with the Ojibwe, who harvested wild rice nearby and fished for sturgeon at the base of the falls.

There are more than 200 sculptures in the Ellsworth Rock Gardens, a unique and popular feature in the park.

After the fur trade died, miners on their way to prospect for gold at Rainy Lake passed through and logging companies sent thousands of cords of harvested timber to Canada, tightly jamming the falls with millions of heavy logs. In 1913, an entrepreneur named Ed Rose built the Kettle Falls Hotel. It was reportedly financed by the intrepid journalist Nellie Bly, who made a record-breaking trip around the world in 72 days. Four years later, a new owner named Robert Williams bought the hotel for $1,000 (about $21,000 today) and four barrels of whiskey. During Prohibition, the hotel was a hot spot for bootleggers who operated distilleries on the property. The legendary red-roofed hotel, which is still open to guests today, is a wonderful way to step out of the busy modern world, especially because it's accessible only by water.

In the winter, the world of Voyageurs is transformed into a white wonderland, where the average annual snowfall is 55 to 70 inches (139.7–177.8 cm)—ideal for skiing and snowshoeing. Out on the lakes the ice can be three feet (0.9 m) thick, prime conditions for snowmobiling from one end of the park to the other. The park even plows a 17-mile-long (27.4 km) ice road navigable by car from the Ash River Visitor Center to the Kabetogama Lake Visitor Center. In the winter especially, the remote park is an excellent vantage point from which to watch the emerald northern lights dance across the sky. In 2020, the International Dark-Sky Association recognized Voyageurs as one of only 80 Dark Sky Parks in the world. ∎

See the Milky Way from your campsite by the lake.

WHAT'S IN A NAME?

For almost two centuries, the fur-transporting tribes in the region used boats they called Voyageur canoes. Modeled after Ojibwe canoes, they were built by wrapping birch bark around a cedar frame and securing it with spruce resin and roots. Each canoe weighed about 300 pounds (136.1 kg), was 25 feet (7.6 m) long and 4 feet (1.2 m) wide, and could carry up to 3,500 pounds (1,360.8 kg).

Seen from the Ash River Visitor
Center, Voyageurs offers stunning
scenery across its waters.

GATEWAY ARCH NATIONAL PARK

★★★★★★★★★★★★★★★★★★★★★★★★

It's hard to miss the Gateway Arch, the 630-foot (192 m) stainless steel sculpture that stands in salute to President Thomas Jefferson and his vision of westward expansionism on the banks of the Mississippi River in downtown St. Louis. Designed by Finnish American architect Eero Saarinen in 1947, the world's tallest arch took two years to construct and was completed in 1965.

The well-built monument seems to transcend every force of nature, designed to sway up to 18 inches (45.7 cm) in 150-mile-an-hour (241.4 km/h) winds and withstand even the most powerful earthquakes.

The less visible component of the Gateway Arch complex, which was designated as a national park in February 2018, is its historic Old Courthouse, where enslaved Dred Scott and his wife, Harriet, sued their owner, Irene Emerson, for their freedom in 1846. Because Missouri courts had previously supported the doctrine of "Once free, always free," Scott and his wife sued on the grounds that they had lived in free territories for years before returning with their owners to St. Louis.

The case dragged on for 11 years, until the Supreme Court ultimately ruled that Scott and his family were not entitled to their freedom. But his courage in filing the lawsuit and his dogged determination to win it was a seminal step in bringing about the Civil War. ■

SIZE OF PARK: .14 square mile (.36 sq km) ★ BEST TIME TO GO: Year-round
YEAR ESTABLISHED: 2018 ★ IN-PARK ACCOMMODATIONS: None

The Gateway Arch stands tall above the park's reflecting pool.

SCOTTS BLUFF NATIONAL MONUMENT

★★★★★★★★★★★★★★★★★★★★★★★★

On the western edge of Nebraska, where the Great Plains give way to the Rocky Mountains, a rock formation juts 800 feet (243.8 m) above the North Platte River. The Cheyenne and Arapaho people who lived here called the sandstone, siltstone, volcanic ash, and limestone escarpment Me-a-pa-te, or "the hill that is hard to go around."

In 1825, a fur-trapping party paddling the North Platte River in canoes arrived at Laramie's Fork, 60 miles (96.6 km) upriver from Me-a-pa-te. They were on the verge of starvation, and one of the men in their party, Hiram Scott, was severely ill. Under the pretense of seeking food, the men abandoned Scott to die. Legend has it that the next summer, some of the original party returned. Sixty miles (96.6 km) downriver, they found a human skull surrounded by bleached white bones. The men determined it to be Scott's and surmised that he had walked or crawled the immense distance before he died at the base of the towering bluff that now bears his name.

In the years of western expansionism throughout the 19th century, Scotts Bluff was a seminal landmark along the 800-mile (1,287.5 km) Great Platte River Road, the "superhighway" used by travelers on several emigrant trails, including the Oregon Trail and the Pony Express. By the time of the 1949 gold rush in California, an estimated 40,000 emigrants traveled 12 to 15 miles (19.3–22.5 km) per day along the route in long wagon trains to start a new future in the West. ■

SIZE OF PARK: 215 square miles (556 sq km) ★ **BEST TIME TO GO:** September to October
YEAR ESTABLISHED: 1971 ★ **IN-PARK ACCOMMODATIONS:** Camping

Prairie schooners sit below the bluff in Mitchell Pass for a reproduction of the Oregon Trail.

THEODORE ROOSEVELT NATIONAL PARK

★★★★★★★★★★★★★★★★★★★★★★★★★

In a letter he wrote to his sister Anna Roosevelt Cowles in 1884, Theodore Roosevelt described the North Dakota Badlands as having "a desolate, grim beauty of its own, that has a curious fascination for me." The 26th president of the United States spent seven years exploring this vast terrain riddled with pastel-hued canyons through which the Little Missouri River flows. Roosevelt hunted bison, ranched cattle, worked as a sheriff for two years, and mourned the sudden deaths of his wife and mother, who perished on the same day in February 1884.

In time, he would increasingly witness the decimation of bison, elk, bighorn sheep, and deer by hunters, and in the brutally harsh winter of 1886–87, he lost 60 percent of his own 1,000 head of cattle. These experiences in the Badlands formed the president's conservation ethic that resulted in his ultimately protecting 230 million acres (93 million ha) of public land while in office.

As lauded as Roosevelt has been for his conservation efforts, little has been written about his view toward Indigenous peoples, which was essentially that they needed to assimilate to the ways of the white man. In creating the park, the federal government effectively took away a portion of the homeland of its Three Affiliated Tribes—the Mandan, Hidatsa, and Arikara Nation—who

SIZE OF PARK: 110 square miles (284 sq km) ★ BEST TIME TO GO: Spring & fall
YEAR ESTABLISHED: 1978 ★ IN-PARK ACCOMMODATIONS: Camping

Bison are what first attracted the president to this landscape.

A rainbow appears after a rainstorm over the hills of the park.

now live on the Fort Berthold Indian Reservation, northeast of the park.

The "grim beauty" that so drew Roosevelt to the Badlands is evident today in the three sections of his namesake park. The dramatic 37.6-square-mile (97.3 sq km) North Unit is where visitors find long backcountry trails framed by the dramatic vistas formed when the Little Missouri was forced to flow east and etch deep into the surrounding sedimentary rock. Thanks to its abundant prairie dog towns, which can be seen from the park road, the 72.1-square-mile South Unit (186.7 sq km) attracts large grazers like bison, elk, and feral horses. At 218-acre (88.2 ha) Elkhorn Ranch, take in the serene site of Roosevelt's low-slung log home, built in 1884 and named after two elk who butted heads, locked horns, and ultimately died of starvation. Only the cornerstones remain, but it's easy to close your eyes and conjure up Roosevelt, sitting on the front porch shaded by towering cottonwoods and overlooking the Missouri River. ■

HIKE OF A LIFETIME

The best way to experience the vast beauty of the Badlands is to backpack the 144-mile-long (231.7 km) Maah Daah Hey Trail, a phrase that means "grandfather" in the Mandan and Hidatsa languages. The trail connects the park's North and South Units, traverses the Little Missouri National Grassland, and crosses the Little Missouri River twice.

CUYAHOGA VALLEY NATIONAL PARK

★★★★★★★★★★★★★★★★★★★★★★★★★★

Centered around the meandering Cuyahoga, or "crooked," River and the thousands of rolling acres of forests and farmlands surrounding it, Ohio's only national park is a tribute to the role transportation played in the transformation of the frontier in the 19th and 20th centuries—from the early days of the Ohio & Erie Canal to the advent of the U.S. interstate system.

Built between 1825 and 1832, the 308-mile-long (496 km) Ohio & Erie Canal provided seamless transportation between Cleveland on Lake Erie south to Portsmouth on the Ohio River. Workers originally from Germany and Ireland tirelessly dug the canal trench for 30 cents per day (about $9.44 today). When they finished, the canal had 146 lift locks and a rise of 1,206 feet (368 m), with an additional five feeder canals that added 24.8 miles (39.9 km) and six additional locks. The resulting corridor was a string of boomtowns that sprung up with mills, taverns, and stores selling fine spices and goods from Europe. Even the canal itself was a community, where boat captains lived on their vessels with their families, the lucky kids dodging school as they made their way downriver.

The canal era ended with the Great Flood of 1913, an unprecedented event that swept away houses, stores, railroad tracks, and even the canal itself. The damage was so extensive that it was deemed too expensive to fix.

SIZE OF PARK: 50.9 square miles (131.8 sq km) ★ **BEST TIME TO GO:** Year-round
YEAR ESTABLISHED: 2000 ★ **IN-PARK ACCOMMODATIONS:** Lodges

Everett Road runs through a historic covered bridge within the park.

To experience the history of the canal and the resulting transformation of the valley, the park maintains roughly 250 historical structures, including the Canal Exploration Center, a onetime store and tavern from the early 1800s, where visitors can listen to John Malvin, a freed Black man, recount his experience as a boat captain; and the fully restored Inn at Brandywine Falls, a Greek Revival home built

The 1.8-mile (2.9 km) Ledges trail circles the striking rock cliffs and giant grassy playfield.

Cascades flow into Brandywine Creek.

Keep a lookout for blue herons in Ohio's only national park.

> 66 Ohio's only national park is a tribute to the role transportation played in the transformation of the frontier in the 19th and 20th centuries. 99

in 1848 overlooking a 67-foot-tall (20.4 m) cascade where park visitors can spend a luxurious night.

Within a one-hour drive of the four million people in the greater Cleveland-Akron-Canton area, Cuyahoga Valley is one of the most visited national parks in the U.S. system. The 140 miles (225.3 km) of hiking, cycling, and horseback-riding trails provide solitude and the chance to glimpse a peregrine falcon or bald eagle, two prevalent raptor species that live in the park. Cycling the Towpath Trail, an 87-mile-long (140 km) paved path, is an excellent way to explore the historic waterway. ■

BADLANDS NATIONAL PARK

★★★★★★★★★★★★★★★★★★★★★★★★★★

For aspiring paleontologists, there is no better place to be than Badlands National Park. Considered the birthplace of vertebrate paleontology in the American West, the Badlands, with their Seussian yellow-brown-and-pale-red buttes, contain layer upon layer of rocks that formed at different moments in geologic time and hold the best preserved snapshot in North America of the transition between the late Eocene epoch (36.9 million years ago) and the late Oligocene epoch (26.8 million years ago).

In 1846, 70 years before the National Park Service existed, one of the first brontothere fossils was discovered in the Badlands within the light gray clay-stone beds of the 37- to 33-million-year-old Chadron Formation. This herbivore, larger than a rhino, had blunt horns at the tip of a three-foot-long (0.9 m) skull and inhabited the lush, hot, wet forests that once covered the region during the late Eocene epoch. In the park's lowest Pierre Shale layer, which is 75 to 69 million years old, fragments of mosasaurs, marine lizards that could grow up to 50 feet (15.2 m) long and lived during the time of the dinosaurs, have been found.

In 2010, a seven-year-old visitor to the park, Kylie Ferguson, saw something interesting poking out of a butte near the Ben Reifel Visitor Center. She left the item where she found it, documented the details, and reported it to a ranger. Her "discovery,"

SIZE OF PARK: 381.25 square miles (987.43 sq km) ★ **BEST TIME TO GO:** April to October
YEAR ESTABLISHED: 1939 ★ **IN-PARK ACCOMMODATIONS:** Lodges & camping

Behold the beauty of the Badlands' colorful mounds and mountain ranges.

In 1922, during the second session of the 67th Congress, South Dakota senator Peter Norbeck introduced legislation entitled "A Bill to Establish the Wonderland National Park in the State of South Dakota." Ultimately, "Wonderland" reverted back to the more appropriate "Badlands," a term the Lakota and French fur trappers used for centuries to describe the area's notoriously wet mud, cold and windy wide-open spaces, and difficult-to-navigate buttes.

which the park knew of but hadn't yet excavated, turned out to be the skull of a carnivorous saber-toothed *Hoplophoneus,* a member of the catlike Nimravidae family. Ferguson's find spurred on the 2012 opening of the Fossil Preparation Lab, a paleontology lab and museum staffed by actual paleontologists that educates visitors in how to properly report fossils they find in the park. In 2019, the lab received 480 site reports from visitors, many of which yielded important new discoveries.

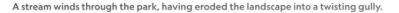

A stream winds through the park, having eroded the landscape into a twisting gully.

But there's a lot more to the Badlands than old bones. Its northern unit contains 64,000 acres (25,899.9 ha) of designated wilderness, a vast landscape of mixed-grass prairies and buttes, where visitors can hike and camp anywhere they choose as long as it's a half mile (0.8 km) away from any road or trail. There are also designated hiking trails that range from the short, steep quarter-mile-long (0.4 km) Saddle Pass Trail with an exhilarating view of the White River Valley to the 10-mile-long (16.1 km) Castle Trail, a relatively flat trail that passes classic Badlands formations.

Once used by the U.S. Air Force as an aerial gunnery range during World War II, the park's South Unit, which is co-managed by the Oglala Sioux Tribe, is open to backcountry campers and hikers today. There are still unexploded bombs, mortars, and other artillery here, so it's wise to check in with park rangers at the White River Visitor Center before heading out into the backcountry.

The park's expansive mixed-grass prairie is home to some very large and very endangered species. The adult bulls in the park's 1,100-strong

Bighorn sheep are often seen throughout the park.

HIDDEN TREASURE

Sod tables, broken segments of grass and soil that are remnants of long-eroding buttes, are common in the park. These flat-topped mounds protect the rock below and also hold 12,000 years of human history, as evidenced by pottery sherds, stone tools, and charcoal fragments found in them.

bison herd can weigh up to 2,000 pounds (907.2 kg) and can run at speeds up to 35 miles an hour (56.3 km/h). Because the bison's natural predators are missing from the park, every year the herd is rounded up and surplus animals are donated to the InterTribal Buffalo Council, a consortium of Native American tribes dedicated to preserving their traditional ties to the buffalo.

An impressive success story in the park is the comeback of the world's most endangered land mammal in North America. The black-footed ferret was declared extinct in 1980, yet because of its aggressive reintroduction program, the park now contains one of the animal's only self-sustaining populations in the world. ∎

Yellow sweet clover dot the grassy meadows at the base of the Badlands' rock formations.

WIND CAVE NATIONAL PARK

★ ★

"Have given up the idea of finding the end of Wind Cave," wrote 17-year-old Alvin Frank McDonald in 1890. As one of the cave's earliest explorers, McDonald found eight to 10 miles (12.9–16.1 km) of passageways by candlelight before he died of typhoid fever in 1893. A century and a quarter later, more than 150 miles (241.4 km) of Wind Cave has been surveyed, which is still only an estimated 10 percent of the entire large and complex cavern—parts of which are 300 million years old—that sits below the Black Hills of South Dakota.

To the Lakota people, whose ancestors have lived in this region for thousands of years, Wind Cave is a sacred entity. Known as Oniya Oshoka, the place where the earth "breathes inside," Wind Cave is where the Lakota emerged from the underground and began their life on earth. When they followed their leader, Tokahe, to the outer world of green hills, blue sky, and bright sunshine, the Lakota saw hoofprints of the bison. Their creator instructed them to follow these hoofprints because, he explained, the bison would give them everything they would need—tools, clothing, food, and shelter—to survive on earth.

Bison are still an integral part of the park's ecosystem, living on the mixed-grass prairie along with pronghorns, coyotes, prairie dogs,

SIZE OF PARK: 52.88 square miles (136.97 sq km) ★ **BEST TIME TO GO:** Year-round
YEAR ESTABLISHED: 1903 ★ **IN-PARK ACCOMMODATIONS:** Camping

Trees dot the vast expanse of green prairie lands throughout Wind River.

Most of us are familiar with cave formations like stalactites and stalagmites, but Wind Cave has more "boxwork" than any other known cave on Earth. This stringy, sci-fi-looking formation is created when thin blades of calcite project from cave walls and ceilings to form a honeycomb pattern that forms shallow "boxes" on cave surfaces.

and elusive burrowing owls. At Sanson Ranch, a homestead site built in the late 1800s that the park recently acquired, there is archaeological evidence of a site where, 4,000 years ago, the Lakota drove herds of bison over a cliff. In the days before horses were introduced to the Lakota by Europeans, driving bison over a cliff was an efficient, albeit exceedingly

Hard to spot, desert cottontails make the park their home.

Wild daisies bloom throughout the park's grasslands.

Nearly 95 percent of the world's boxwork formations are found in Wind Cave, one of the densest cave systems.

dangerous, way to hunt. Just one successful "jump" could feed, clothe, and shelter the Lakota for an entire year.

Above- or belowground, there is much to explore at Wind Cave, one of the oldest national parks in the country. Enjoy 30 miles (48.3 km) of hiking trails that take in the mixed-grass prairie and surrounding ponderosa pine forests. For those who want to descend into the abyss, park rangers lead guided cave tours, the most extensive of which is four hours long and involves crawling. ■

66 Above- or belowground, there is much to explore at Wind Cave. 99

APOSTLE ISLANDS NATIONAL LAKESHORE

★★★★★★★★★★★★★★★★★★★★★★★★★

Of the estimated 35,000 islands in the Great Lakes, there are only 400 in mighty Lake Superior. That's why the sheltering bays and sandy anchorages of the Apostle Islands, a 22-island archipelago off northwestern Wisconsin's Bayfield Peninsula, are ideal for kayakers and sailors who want to safely explore the world's largest freshwater lake (when measured by surface area).

Twenty-one of the 22 islands make up Apostle Islands National Lakeshore, which also includes a 12-mile (19.3 km) coastal strip of mainland. The exception is Madeline Island, the largest in the archipelago, at 15,359 acres (6,215.6 ha). Called *Mooniingwanekaaning-minis,* or "Home of the Yellow-Breasted Woodpecker," it has long been an important spiritual and cultural homeland for the Ojibwe people. Collectively the islands are known as *Wenabozho ominisan* ("Wenabozho's islands"), taken from a story about how the Ojibwe cultural hero, Wenabozho, created them.

All the Apostle Islands are sacred to the Ojibwe. Their natural beauty and power are evident from the thick forests of yellow birch, sugar maple, balsam fir, and hemlock on 8,000-acre (3,237.5 ha) Outer Island, which lies 25 miles (40.2 km) off the mainland to the sandstone sea caves—which kayakers can explore when the lake is calm—that then turn into magical jaws of ice during the coldest winters.

SIZE OF PARK: 108 square miles (281 sq km) ★ **BEST TIME TO GO:** June to September
YEAR ESTABLISHED: 1970 ★ **IN-PARK ACCOMMODATIONS:** Camping

Though often inaccessible, the ice caves along Lake Superior are a one-of-a-kind experience.

While most of the islands today are designated wilderness, the Apostles have witnessed many eras of human history dating back thousands of years, to when the first Indigenous people once thrived in the area thanks to an abundance of resources found throughout the islands. The most evident human markers are the seven light stations scattered across the islands. These beautifully crafted structures, like the Italianate white stucco lighthouse on Outer Island, were built in the 1800s to aid increasing ship traffic on the frightfully powerful lake.

The best way to explore the island is by boat. Today, GPS is the most common navigational tool, but it's a good idea to bring a map and compass. There are sandy anchorages and safe harbors, but those looking for an adventure here need to understand that Lake Superior's average annual temperature is 42°F (5.5°C). Locals say "the lake is the boss" for good reason. Sea conditions change very quickly. That's why it's essential to be prepared, check the latest weather conditions, especially wind forecasts, and be flexible with plans. ∎

RARE SIGHTING

The winter ice formations in the mainland sea caves are a dazzling sight, with frozen waterfalls and daggers of ice suspended from the rock. The only way to access the caves is to hike almost two miles (3.2 km) on the frozen ice of Lake Superior, though many factors can contribute to the trek being deemed unsafe. The last time they could be safely reached was in 2015.

Take in the Apostle Islands' unique rock formations on a paddling excursion through Lake Superior.

PROTECT OUR PARKS

Parks are invaluable oases that are essential to our well-being, giving us the freedom we crave to roam, explore, and play. They are also increasingly vulnerable to the effects of climate change, overcrowding, underfunding, and the cultural and environmental degradation that comes with ignorance.

We all want our parks to last for generations to come. But paying an entrance fee, if one is even required, isn't enough to ensure that our parks will be protected and maintained. Here are nine ways we can all help to shoulder the load and ensure our parks survive:

1. **Get Educated.** Every park in the nation possesses unique cultural history, geology, geography, and wildlife. Every park also has unique stressors to its ecosystems. Do your research. Understand the environment you are choosing to enter and what is required from you as a visitor. The National Park Service, the U.S. Forest Service, and most other organizations that manage parks and public lands have extensive online resources. Read the park's rules and regulations, the frequently asked questions, and its cultural and natural history so that you have a better understanding and appreciation for the people who came before the park and how the park itself came to be.

2. **Plan Ahead.** Spontaneously winging it when visiting the country's most popular parks is a luxury of the past, especially during the busiest summer months. As of 2021, Glacier National Park instituted an online reservation system for driving the Going-to-the-Sun Road between May and September. Other parks, like Yosemite, require visitors to enter an online lottery for hiking iconic trails like Half Dome. And many parks require reservations months in advance for staying overnight in their most popular campgrounds and lodges. These are wise and necessary changes, but be aware of these restrictions and consider planning a trip in the off-season, which will help better distribute visitors.

3. **Follow Rules.** Rules are there for a reason. Follow them. One great example for doing so: Soils in some places like Utah's Canyonlands National Park are so delicate that stepping off the trail can do decades', if not centuries', worth of damage. Heed the signs imploring visitors to stay on the trail.

4. **Vote.** The single most effective way to make your voice heard is to vote at every level—city, county, state, and federal—for politicians who prioritize legislation and funds that protect

our parks. Even if your candidate doesn't win, it's still important to stay engaged, calling and writing, to raise your voice in opposition.

5. **Give Back.** Your time, expertise, and financial resources—whether you volunteer to maintain trails, serve on a park board, or donate money to a nonprofit that funds your favorite park—are invaluable contributions. Identify your particular gifts and use them to help the parks.

6. **Leave No Trace.** Many parks have seen an exponential increase in visitation over the past few years. That has also meant an exponential increase in garbage, human waste, and other human impacts. "Leave no trace" may seem like a no-brainer, but educate yourself about how to best carry out that mandate in every environment, whether that means cleaning up after your dog in a city park, picking the charred scraps of marshmallow off the fire grate at your campsite, or packing out everything you packed in on a multi-day wilderness trip.

7. **Be Self-Aware.** Disturbances take many shapes when sharing public spaces. Some may think it's perfectly within their rights to pull their car over by the side of the road to snap a quick shot of a roaming buffalo, blocking traffic for miles; or to stay up until midnight singing songs around a campfire; or to talk loudly to a companion when hiking down a trail. But your actions affect other humans, as well as wildlife, so give other visitors and wildlife the dignity and distance they deserve.

8. **Take Public Transportation.** Whether taking a subway across town to visit Central Park, taking a train across the country to visit a national park, or taking a shuttle within the park once you've arrived, fewer cars on the road means decreased traffic congestion, fewer parking problems, and less exhaust and noise pollution. Once inside the parks, most shuttles are free and take you exactly where you need to go.

9. **Explore Your Own Backyard.** Before you hop a jet across the country for a weekend get-away, consider the impacts of your actions. Is there a way to mitigate the carbon required to get you there? Can you plan the journey in a way that allows you to maximize your time and minimize future trips to the same destination? Could you get even better rest and relaxation by planning a trip closer to home that requires fewer resources to get there?

ACKNOWLEDGMENTS

Parks and other public lands have offered me space, solitude, and freedom at the times in life I needed it most. I owe more than a debt of gratitude to their original inhabitants.

No park experience would be possible today if it weren't for the visionaries who recognized the intrinsic value of these landscapes and acted to protect them. Thank you also to the employees, past and present, whose knowledge, stewardship, and hard work make these places accessible to everyone; the scientists whose research helps to further their evolution; the nonprofit organizations and volunteers whose time and fundraising efforts enhance the parks; and to the elected officials who prioritize wild spaces over extractive legislation.

Writing a book about 100 different locations is a fact-intensive mission. Thank you to all historians, scientists, and public information officers who helped me navigate the intricacies of each park and fact-check details. I also thank friends and colleagues who provided personal experience and expertise on parks that I did not have the opportunity to visit during the pandemic.

National Geographic is the first magazine I read as a child. It continues to delight and amaze me. Thank you to Editor in Chief Susan Goldberg and her staff for challenging me to think big. More specifically, thanks to Allyson Johnson and Lisa Gerry for your grace and kindness in the writing and editing process; and to copy editor Jacqueline Hornberger for your painstakingly careful work. I'm also grateful for the design team, photo editor Jill Foley, designer Jennifer Gibson Frink, art director Sanaa Akkach, director of photography Susan Blair, and senior production editor Judith Klein, for creating such a beautiful, inviting book. Heartfelt thanks to all the editors I've worked with at National Geographic over the years, including George Stone, Amy Alipio, Brooke Sabin, Norie Quintos, Oliver Payne, and Anne Farrar, who have supported and encouraged me.

My journalism career began at *Outside* magazine in 1995. I am deeply appreciative of my editors there, especially Mary Turner, Chris Keyes, Hal Espen, Mark Bryant, and Susan Casey, who have given me the opportunity to explore the world, including many of these parks.

A thank-you isn't nearly enough to express the gratitude I feel toward my mom and late dad for instilling in me a deep love and respect for the outdoors. A salute to my siblings, Jen, Scott, Jon, and Tim, for being my first playmates in many great park escapades right up the street. And to Brian, my partner in life, thank you for your love, patience, and curiosity.

PARKS BY STATE

ILLUSTRATIONS CREDITS

Cover, Mark Brodkin Photography/Getty Images; 2-3, Gordon Wiltsie; 4-5, Per Breiehagen/Getty Images; 7, Jason Savage/TandemStock; 9, Denis Tangney Jr/Getty Images; 10-11, Laurie Chamberlain/Getty Images; 12-13, Brent Clark Photography/Getty Images; 14-15, benedek/Getty Images; 17, Ian Shive/TandemStock; 19, Mike Theiss; 20, John Burcham; 21, Pete McBride; 22-3, Pete McBride/National Geographic Image Collection; 25, Ian Shive/TandemStock; 26, Rich Leighton; 27 (LE), Ian Shive/TandemStock; 27 (RT), Jack Dykinga/NPL/Minden Pictures; 29, Miles Morgan/TandemStock; 30-1, Alex Treadway; 33, NPS/Emily Hassell; 34, NPS/Hannah Schwalbe; 35, Whitney Tressel; 37, Nathan Hadley/TandemStock; 38 (LE), Peter Carey/Alamy Stock Photo; 38 (RT), Pam Susemiehl/Getty Images; 39, sierralara/Getty Images; 41, Patrick Leitz/Getty Images; 43, Kaare Iverson/TandemStock; 44, Phil Schermeister; 45 (LE), George Ostertag/Alamy Stock Photo; 45 (RT), NPS/Kurt Moses; 47, Modoc Stories/robertharding; 48, YayaErnst/Getty Images; 49, Matt Propert; 51, Michael Nichols/National Geographic Image Collection; 53, Simon Roberts/National Geographic Image Collection; 54, Sergio Pitamitz; 55, Neil Losin/Day's Edge Productions LLC/TandemStock; 56-7, cdrin/Shutterstock; 59, Axel Brunst/TandemStock; 60, Lee Rentz/Alamy Stock Photo; 61, Ian Shive/TandemStock; 62-3, James Shive/TandemStock; 65, Adam Burton/robertharding; 66, Marc Moritsch; 67, David Hoffmann Photography/robertharding; 68-9, Robb Hirsch/TandemStock; 71, Mountain Girl Photography/Cavan Images; 72, dschnarrs/Getty Images; 73, Justin Bailie/TandemStock; 75, Lisa J Godfrey; 77, Peter Unger/Getty Images; 78, Cheri Alguire/Getty Images; 79 (LE), Spring Images/Alamy Stock Photo; 79 (RT), Jim West/Alamy Stock Photo; 81, Paul Hamill/TandemStock; 82-3, Ronda Kimbrow Photography/Getty Images; 85, Leon Werdinger/Alamy Stock Photo; 86, Greg Vaughn/Alamy Stock Photo; 87 (LE), Boyd Norton/Alamy Stock Photo; 87 (RT), Christian Nafzger/Getty Images; 89, Ray Urner/TandemStock; 90, Raul Touzon; 91, Kelly Cheng Travel Photography/Getty Images; 92-3, Bryan Jolley/TandemStock; 95, Jordan Banks/robertharding; 96 (LE), Evgeny Vasenev/Cavan/Getty Images; 96 (RT), Jason Savage/TandemStock; 97, KHaker/Getty Images; 99, Paolo Negri/age fotostock; 100, powerofforever/Getty Images; 101, EWY Media/Shutterstock Editorial; 103, Tristan Brynildsen/Alamy Stock Photo; 104, Rachid Dahnoun/TandemStock; 105, Chuck Haney/DanitaDelimont/Alamy Stock Photo; 107, Robbie Shone; 109, Dawn Kish; 110, R. Tyler Gross/Cavan/Getty Images; 111, Derek von Briesen; 113, Phil Degginger/Alamy Stock Photo; 114, Ed Callaert/Alamy Stock Photo; 115 (LE), R. Tyler Gross/Cavan/Getty Images; 115 (RT), Bill Gorum/Alamy Stock Photo; 117, Jeff Lewis/TandemStock; 118, Cavan Images/Isaac Lane Koval/Getty Images; 119 (LE), Thomas Winz/Getty Images; 119 (RT), Michael Rooney/

Alamy Stock Photo; 121, 4FR/Getty Images; 122 (LE), Leamus/Getty Images; 122 (RT), Jeff Foott/Minden Pictures; 123, Ben Horton; 125, Brad McGinley Photography/Getty Images; 126, Cavan Images/Peter Lobozzo/Getty Images; 127 (LE), Tetra Images/robert harding; 127 (RT), Mark Meredith/Getty Images; 129, jenifoto/Getty Images; 131, Posnov/Getty Images; 132, Grant Ordelheide/TandemStock; 133 (LE), David Pickford/robertharding; 133 (RT), Lynn Wegener/robert harding; 135, Kirk Mastin/Cavan Images; 136 (LE), Dennis Frates/Alamy Stock Photo; 136 (RT), Natures ThumbPrint/Getty Images; 137, Jordan Banks/TandemStock; 139, Colin Brynn/robertharding; 140, Marc Pagani/Cavan Images; 141 (LE), Woodward/Cardy/Alamy Stock Photo; 141 (RT), Chase Dekker/Minden Pictures; 143, Michael Hanson; 145, Jordan Siemens/Getty Images; 146, Stephen Matera/TandemStock; 147 (LE), Art Wolfe/robertharding; 147 (RT), Raul Touzon; 149, J.C. Leacock/Cavan Images; 150, Charlie Hamilton James/National Geographic Image Collection; 151, Ben Herndon/TandemStock; 152-3, crbellette/Getty Images; 154-5, Michael Melford/National Geographic Image Collection; 157, Carl Johnson/robertharding; 158, Cavan Images/Daniel A. Sands/Getty Images; 159, Carl Johnson/Design Pics Inc/Alamy Stock Photo; 160-1, Corey Rich/Cavan Images/Alamy Stock Photo; 163, Spencer Clark/robertharding; 164, Steven Miley/Design Pics Inc; 165 (LE), PhotoSpirit/Alamy Stock Photo; 165 (RT), Aaron Huey/National Geographic Image Collection; 167, Katie Orlinsky; 168, Patrick J Endres/AlaskaPhotoGraphics; 169 (LE), Carl Johnson/Getty Images; 169 (RT), Patrick J Endres/AlaskaPhotoGraphics; 171, Frans Lanting; 172, Ethan Welty/TandemStock; 173, Cappan/Getty Images; 175, Brent Doscher/Cavan Images; 176, Michael Melford; 177 (LE), ML Harris/Alamy Stock Photo; 177 (RT), Peter Carey/Alamy Stock Photo; 179, Gfed/Getty Images; 180, CS Nafzger/Shutterstock; 181, Ralph Lee Hopkins; 183, James + Courtney Forte/Getty Images; 185, Nick Jans/Design Pics Inc/Alamy Stock Photo; 186 (LE), Doug Demarest/Design Pics Inc/Alamy Stock Photo; 186 (RT), Nick Jans/Design Pics Inc/Alamy Stock Photo; 187, Natural History Library/Alamy Stock Photo; 189, Tandem Stills + Motion/Ian Shive/Getty Images; 190 (LE), Jonathan Irish; 190 (RT), Jonathan Irish; 191, Michael Runkel/DanitaDelimont/Alamy Stock Photo; 193, NPS Photo; 195, Jim Willschko/Getty Images; 196, Joshua Rainey/robertharding; 197, Sami Sarkis/Getty Images; 198-9, Ian Shive/TandemStock; 201, Peter French/Design Pics Inc; 203, Fabian Meseberg/EyeEm/Getty Images; 204, Aaron Black-Schmidt/TandemStock; 205 (LE), Raphael Rivest/Shutterstock; 205 (RT), Rich Reid; 207, MC2 Charles Oki/US Navy/Alamy Stock Photo; 208 (LE), PantherMedia/GlowImages/Alamy Stock Photo; 208 (RT), Insa Hagemann/laif/Redux; 209, SeregaSibTravel/Shutterstock Editorial; 211, Laurie Chamberlain/Getty Images; 212, Michael Runkel/

ABOUT THE AUTHOR

STEPHANIE PEARSON is a contributing editor to *Outside* magazine and a freelance writer. Her assignments over three decades have included reporting from Mount Everest Base Camp, meditating with Tibetan Buddhist scholar Bob Thurman in Bhutan, and producing a real-time online science curriculum for middle-school students while traveling through Australia and Latin America with National Geographic Fellow Dan Buettner and his team.

After receiving her master's degree from Northwestern University's Medill School of Journalism, Pearson began her career at *Outside,* where she was on the editorial staff for more than a decade. Pearson has received a number of Lowell Thomas Awards from the Society of American Travel Writers Foundation in the categories of Foreign Travel, Environmental and Sustainable Tourism, Service-Oriented Consumer Work, and Travel Journalist of the Year. Her features have also been anthologized in the Best American Travel Writing series and *Out There: The Wildest Stories from* Outside *Magazine.*

Pearson lives in northern Minnesota, where she tries to fully embrace the four seasons, even on subzero days. Find her on Twitter @stephanieapears, on Instagram @stephanieapearson, or on her website: stephanieannpearson.com.

Since 1888, the National Geographic Society has funded more than 14,000 research, conservation, education, and storytelling projects around the world. National Geographic Partners distributes a portion of the funds it receives from your purchase to National Geographic Society to support programs including the conservation of animals and their habitats.

Get closer to National Geographic Explorers and photographers, and connect with our global community. Join us today at nationalgeographic.org/joinus

For rights or permissions inquiries, please contact National Geographic Books Subsidiary Rights: bookrights@natgeo.com

Library of Congress Cataloging-in-Publication Data
Names: Pearson, Stephanie, 1970 - author. | Brooks, Garth, author of foreword.
Title: 100 great American parks / Stephanie Pearson; foreword by Garth Brooks.
Other titles: One hundred great American parks
Description: Washington, D.C.: National Geographic, [2022] | Includes index.
Summary: "This beautifully illustrated collection highlights America's 62 national parks and 38 state, recreational, and city parks and green spaces"-- Provided by publisher.
Identifiers: LCCN 2021029429 | ISBN 9781426222009 (hardcover)
Subjects: LCSH: National parks and reserves--United States--Guidebooks.
National parks and reserves--United States--History. | Parks--United States--Guidebooks.
Classification: LCC E160 .P43 2022 | DDC 917.304/934--dc23

LC record available at https://lccn.loc.gov/2021029429

ISBN: 978-1-4262-2200-9

Printed in China

22/RRDH/1

The information in this book has been carefully checked and to the best of our knowledge is accurate. However, details are subject to change, and the publisher cannot be responsible for such changes, or for errors or omissions. Assessments of sites, hotels, and restaurants are based on the author's subjective opinions, which do not necessarily reflect the publisher's opinion.

I EXPLORE OUR NATIONAL PARKS

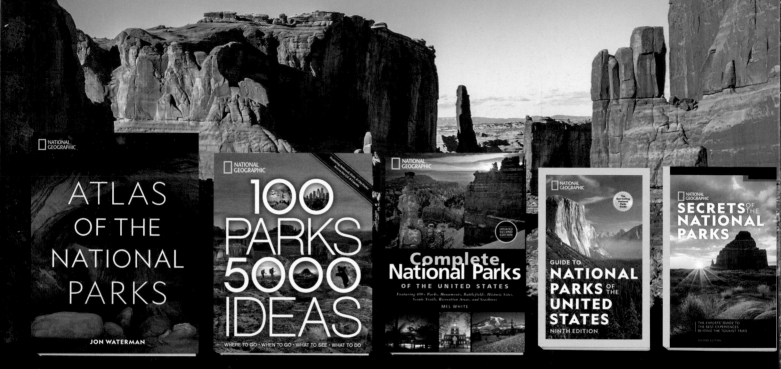

ATLAS OF THE NATIONAL PARKS — JON WATERMAN

100 PARKS 5000 IDEAS — WHERE TO GO · WHEN TO GO · WHAT TO SEE · WHAT TO DO

Complete National Parks OF THE UNITED STATES — MEL WHITE

GUIDE TO NATIONAL PARKS OF THE UNITED STATES — NINTH EDITION

SECRETS OF THE NATIONAL PARKS

FOR KIDS

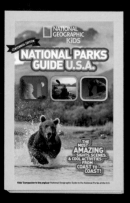

NATIONAL PARKS GUIDE U.S.A. — THE MOST AMAZING SIGHTS, SCENES, & COOL ACTIVITIES FROM COAST TO COAST!

National Parks of the United States

MORE THAN 50 NATIONAL PARKS MAPS!

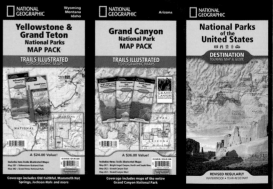

Yellowstone & Grand Teton National Parks MAP PACK — TRAILS ILLUSTRATED TOPOGRAPHIC MAPS — A $24.00 Value! — Coverage includes Old Faithful, Mammoth Hot Springs, Jackson Hole and more

Grand Canyon National Park MAP PACK — TRAILS ILLUSTRATED TOPOGRAPHIC MAPS — A $36.00 Value! — Coverage includes maps of the entire Grand Canyon National Park

National Parks of the United States DESTINATION TOURING MAP & GUIDE — REVISED REGULARLY — WATERPROOF · TEAR-RESISTANT

I AVAILABLE WHEREVER BOOKS ARE SOLD

f NatGeoBooks   @NatGeoBooks

NATIONAL GEOGRAPHIC